KNOWING YOURSELF

- ❖ Define Your Personality
- ❖ Interpret Other Personalities
- ❖ Enhance Your Love Life
- ❖ Understand Your Natural Defenses
- ❖ Accept the "Real You"

By
Virginia Schroeder Burnham
in collaboration with
William H. Hampton, M.D.

SUNDIAL
PUBLICATIONS

First Edition
Printed in the United States of America

———

Library of Congress Cataloging-in-Publication Data:
Burnham, Virginia Schroeder, 1908-
    Knowing yourself / by Virginia Schroeder Burnham, in collaboration with William H. Hampton. — 1st ed.
       p. cm.
    Includes index.
    ISBN 0-86534-151-6 : $14.95
    1. Self-perception. 2. Typology (psychology) 3. Adjustment (psychology)
I. Hampton, William H., 1925- . II. Title.
BF697 . 5.S43B84 1992
155.2—dc20   92-4733
                                 CIP

Published by   Sunstone Press
                    Post Office Box 2321
                    Santa Fe, NM 87504-2321 / USA

CONTENTS

PREFACE

We feel strongly that people have a need for information on how the mind works, and that everyone has a right to know the truth. We are not promoting a new scheme, nor disproving existing concepts. Our objective is to interpret the intricacies of the makeup of personality in language that is candid and understandable.

This book is based on intensive research of the literature in conjunction with the authors' life experiences and over thirty years of psychiatric practice. We give facts gleaned from years of observation by professionals and the long experience of leaders in psychiatry and the behavioral sciences. We give facts that we know to be true based on scientific studies, and facts we consider to be true. And we acknowledge ignorance where we don't know.

If this book fulfills our purpose:

You will be able to detect the hang-ups you have and learn how to free yourself from them.

You will learn what makes other people tick, and why they do as they do, and don't think and act as you do.

You will be able to recognize the mental quirks, idiosyncrasies and puzzling ways of others, name them and understand and accept them.

You will be able to recognize personality defects and know what can be done about them.

In short, you will come to know yourself and others better, especially those closest to you, improve your association with them and create more compatible relationships.

We believe that the public lacks reliable information on these subjects, and we want to set the record straight. What most people know is learned from others and gathered from the media. What they may not know is that up to fifty percent of the population is in need of counseling or psychiatric care, and most who receive it are cured or improved sufficiently to live normal lives.

Note that we use the words "thinking" and "doing" which, for clarity, we have substituted for the technical terms "schizoid" and "psychopathic." "Schizoid, or thinking; is chemical and "psychopathic," doing or acting out, is electrical. When we think, we utilize chemical substances in the brain, when we do, or act out, we utilize electrical activity in the brain. Thus, life is made up of the chemical thinking and the electrical doing.

As the word "schizoid" is not understood by the average layman and can be confused with schizophrenia, which is a thinking illness, we use thinking. As the term "psychopathic" is regarded as something abnormal and relates to movement, we use doing or acting out. Doing may be benevolent or evil, but is not necessarily unhealthy.

So, we have both thinking and doing, and these two elements, combined in varying degrees, form our personalities, supported by intelligence and energy. These four are the fundamental blocks of every personality. When we understand them, we can understand ourselves, and direct our lives to what are for us the most advantageous and positive areas.

INTRODUCTION

Y ou ask, why should I read this book? The answer is simple, to become better acquainted with your personality. And by knowing yourself, you will learn how to know others better, and life will be less complicated.

There have been many books written on personality but I guarantee that there is none that is as explicit and easy to read as this one. It was written by a lay person for the lay person who wants the facts about personality in an understandable language. I have felt for a long time that there is a need for this knowledge, and I can attest that learning about myself while working on it has influenced my life immeasurably. I can now understand the guilt and fears I suffered needlessly, and that certain thoughts I had and deeds I committed that I was ashamed of are not wrong, but only human. My self-image has become enhanced to the extent that I can hold my head high, and I trust that you also will benefit from the knowledge I acquired and which you will find in this book.

You will learn where your personality came from and what its makeup is, how your brain works and how to use it to your advantage. You will recognize the talents you were born with and that you can develop any skill you want to, and that the use of preventive techniques through life is the key to achieving the heights to which you aspire. You will find out what influences were responsible in shaping your personality and how to overcome the bad characteristics you have and capitalize on the good ones. However, we cannot change our personalities to the extent of eliminating traits we wish we didn't have, nor can we acquire those we don't have, but we can influence them all by building up those we like and subduing those we don't.

We tell you the difference between instincts we are born with and habits which we form, and the similarity of our instincts to those of animals and other living creatures. We explain how we form habits because we are taught to or have to, and sometimes form them inadvertently.

This book explains sexuality and the practices of men and women in regard to intercourse and the other aspects of sex. It treats this pervasive area of our lives in sensitive detail, its possibilities, innuendos and ramifications.

You will become acquainted with the attributes we all possess, such as paranoia, and learn what that means and how it is woven inextricably into the way we conduct our lives. You will understand why some people are very untidy, some excessively tidy, and why you prefer to pursue a regular routine or would rather adhere to a hit-and-miss schedule.

You will find that it is never too late to develop the talents you were born with and to brush up on the skills you have perfected, no matter how long ago. We tell you how men and women are different and about likes and dislikes. You will understand why you have dreams and that daydreaming is beneficial and OK to practice. We explain why you have physical complaints off and on and what to do about them, and that being neurotic is normal and in some ways helpful to your well-being. And there is much, much more.

I trust you will enjoy this little book and glean from it information you can use to your advantage.

Virginia Schroeder Burnham
Greenwich, Connecticut
July 1992

1

THE MAKEUP OF PERSONALITY

What is personality? Do you know what yours is like? Your personality is the outward sign of your inner self. It is comprised of emotional, intellectual and physical qualities intricately interwoven into the person that is YOU. It is the awareness of being apart from others and the realization that everyone has that same awareness. It is a quest for identity unique to man and inseparable from self-conscious existence. It is the hallmark of a man or woman striving to become fully human.

Personality is mental power which controls abilities and capabilities—what you think, and the way you use your mind, what you do and how you do it. Why are you different from other people and think and do as you do? It is how you feel, sad or happy, depressed or elated, angry or loving, well or sick. All can change as quickly as a wink. It is the way you look, the way you move and stand and use your hands and feet—body, mind and spirit working as one. And a lot more.

Where does personality come from? According to early theory, personality is formed during childhood by the environment and the circumstances into which a person is born; the kind of family, the customs, the location, the schooling, the upbringing. Most modern thinking, however, maintains that the basic qualities of personality are born with us and don't change throughout life. We believe that neither of these concepts is entirely correct. We believe that personality is formed by a combination of heredity and the effects of the environment, and that heredity is the most important. Personality may be influenced by circumstances, but there is convincing evidence that basic qualities are inborn. The family, the school, the upbringing and the quality of the setting have a great deal of impact on what we learn as a child.

The issue of personality formation has been a raging argument for decades. It is called the "nature or nurture" controversy. Believers in Freudian psychiatry stick to nurture, the environment; believers in biological psychiatry adhere to nature, heredity. The dispute won't be resolved until scientific evidence establishes the truth.

Your personality is YOU and it is unique. It has never been duplicated and never will be. It is your heritage and stays with you through life. No two people are created alike, not even identical twins. This individuality is one of the laws of nature and applies to all forms of life, whether they be animals, birds, fish, flowers or trees. Even snowflakes are not alike.

We don't inherit traits directly. We are not necessarily like our parents, or even our grandparents. Rather, personality is a mixture of genes going back many generations, perhaps thousands of years. Hence we are essentially different from our parents, as our children are from us, although we may have traits in common. Our children may be more like a grandparent or a great-grandparent than they are like us, but they will be more like us than the Joneses next door. As human beings we share every personality characteristic, good and bad. In this way only, are we similar. The amounts vary from person to person, and this is what makes us unique.

A personality has four cornerstones: thinking, doing, intelligence and energy. We are born with these elements in varying degrees; each can be high, low or in between. They cannot be measured exactly, but we can easily pick out a person with high intelligence or high energy (which is the same as drive) because these elements are so obvious. To determine the degree of thinking and doing is more difficult, except in extreme cases. So it is possible to determine our own personality and figure out what makes others tick. However, this takes a special insight.

As you examine your own, you may find you are more of a thinker than a doer, or vice versa, you may have high intelligence and low energy or the reverse; more likely, you are somewhere in between. So you need to evaluate each characteristic on a scale of one to ten. In addition, you have passive and aggressive traits and obsessive and compulsive feelings, which stay in the background until you face a situation that forces their use. Personality also includes sexuality and the quality of paranoia, which we will describe. So these basic qualities are inherited and don't change throughout life, although experience, education and the environment play a part in modifying, enhancing or repressing them.

Here are the four cornerstones:

Intelligence
Thinking   Doing
Energy

The thinking and doing are balanced and closely related, each struggling for control. We can't function without both, however, as they are dependent on one another, and helpless when separated, such as when we are asleep. Then, our movements (doing) and thinking are random and not goal directed. Thus, we cannot move without some thinking and, when thinking, plan some sort of doing, like writing, walking or speaking, causing activity inside brain cells. This is why both doing and thinking cause fatigue. These cells have chemical and electrical components, and thinking is stimulated by the chemical and doing by the electrical. Personality is determined by the predominance of thinking or doing, but always influenced by intelligence and energy.

THINKING AND DOING

Thinking is the working of the mentation areas of the brain, while doing is the movements of the body controlled by the action areas of the body. Many human problems are caused by efforts to coordinate the two. We have control, but not total control. For instance, we can bring thoughts to mind but suddenly they can be crowded out by an unrelated thought, the telephone or some trivial matter, and it takes considerable effort to return to the original subject. The same is true of doing, such as when we stop a task before it is completed to do something else.

Animals have these same characteristics and it is amusing and entertaining to watch our two cats who came into our family as kittens. As they developed, we could easily determine that one is a thinker and the other a doer. Veronica, the thinker, is into everything, investigating and sniffing at every object and corner in the house. She is not as friendly as Victoria, who is affectionate and bouncy. She likes people and is not particularly interested in finding out about things. It is interesting to observe that the thinking and doing elements apply also to animals.

Let's examine the thinking side further. It is sensitive, intro-verted and idealistic. It likes creative activities: painting, designing, modeling, engineering, building. It is the quality that wants to be alone, to read and study, and to focus on details. It is the mathemati-cal part that is oriented toward objects. A predominantly thinking person relates to things more easily than to people and enjoys using the mind. For example, more of a thinker likes to be alone, to work alone, and resents being interrupted. When there is too much solitude, the doing side rebels. Suddenly, restlessness sets in and the thinker craves to see people and enjoy a little fun. This happens when the thinking side is allowed to take over and if the thinker submits to that impulse, his mood is greatly improved.

It's hard for most of us to get out of bed in the morning and sometimes we awaken to a low mood. The mood swings up and down according to multiple factors and seldom stays on an even keel. Everyone is different as to how high or low it goes and what causes it to fluctuate. Some people are "even tempered" and sail through life with minimal ups and downs, some are always a little up, some always a little down. These last are the negative thinkers who are slightly depressed, unhappy people.

The mind is always busy while awake. How we think deter-mines how we act. We can train our minds to work for us or let it control us. Thinkers are more apt to be moody with swings up and down. Doers are most often happy-go-lucky, bouncy, and cheerful, with few down moments.

A long time ago, Eleanor Porter wrote a book on thinking positively. The story was about a young girl called Pollyanna who always looked on the bright side of things. She was a happy child, in fact, she was optimistic even in dire circumstances, and to be a "Pollyanna" became a common expression. Negative thinking is a depressant, positive a stimulant, and mood is the dominant force behind these opposing ways of thinking. Health influences mood, which is low during illness, and negative thoughts prevail. The high energy person can ride over the negatives, while the low energy person overlooks the positives and becomes depressed. It is difficult to control mood. One way to make it swing up is by exercising, for exercise changes the chemistry of brain cells. We hear of the "runner's high." That is what happens when we feel elated after running past the point of initial fatigue and reach a euphoric plateau.

Here is an example of how the mind reacts to exercise. When my daughter was in Junior High, she came home from school on the bus, dropped her books and ran around the house three or four times. When asked why, she said, "I have to get the cobwebs out of my brain." Instinct told her to blow off steam, and the doing relaxed the thinking which had been working hard all day, resulting in an imbalance. A change of pace gets the same result, such as a lively conversation or reading an interesting book. This corrects the imbalance.

Do your thoughts ever shock you? Do you ever feel like killing someone who has wronged you, and express to yourself: "I could kill him!"? Perhaps you swear and find it slightly comforting. Why? Because you are releasing your anger. These reactions are human and healthy, the civilized way of fighting back. It is important to express anger for, if you keep it inside, you will develop depression and perhaps physical illness, such as headaches, stomach ulcers, or a low resistance to disease. Expressing anger ventilates the mind and can take many forms, such as an outburst of swear words, throwing something or pouring out your feelings to a friend. Exercising vigorously can also get anger out of your system and you will feel much better.

Anger creates another kind of battle within the brain. When we get mad, how do we show it? Usually in a way that reflects our personality and sophistication. The disciplined person may turn to exercise in some form, such as vehemently mopping the floor or chopping wood. This works like magic, but few of us are that well organized. If we lack self control or allow it to relax, we use the primitive approach, which is a verbal or even a physical attack. But anger doesn't just go away, but often is dissipated by directing it elsewhere, such as the discord at home is taken out at the office and the controversy at work rebounds on the family.

However, anger is not unhealthy, nor is it wrong. On the contrary, it is appropriate for both men and women as a normal response which should be respected and released in a fitting manner. What is unhealthy is to deny anger and not allow it to vent itself, for anger just does not evaporate. It is transformed into physical or emotional release and, if it is not allowed to be expressed in some way, will turn into depression. Women dislike physical violence, guns, knives and the like, but some women are subject to feelings of aggressive and violence as are men, but they take it out in a different way, usually verbally or by sneaky, manipulative acts. So anger results in some activity, it always changes into something, and may go away in a minute or a week, a month or a year. Sometimes it stays for a long time.

So anger is unavoidable and is especially difficult for mothers, because children are going to fight, especially boys, due to their stronger aggressive instinct. However, if they are forced to control anger, it will be bottled up inside, and this can bring on depression or physical symptoms. The anger comes out sooner or later and in primitive forms, for children are primitive.

Children release their anger more often than adults. We understand this because we realize they have little control, but when a disagreement breaks out in physical violence or vicious words, we are quick to discipline. However, this implants inhibitions in the more thinking child and removes them from the more doing. So, as anger will not just disappear, parents must find out what produced it and take steps to resolve the controversy that started it. Most parents find it difficult to compromise with children and wait too long to intervene, or jump in immediately with commands. Either does more harm than good.

How do children react to anger? The thinking child takes it out in a thinking way, like building a fantasy in which he overthrows his adversary, or he may plot revenge in a sneaky fashion, such as letting the air out of his opponent's bicycle tires. The doing child does something more obvious, such as holding his breath, throwing a tantrum or deliberately breaking something. These reactions are healthy, and each child has a way that is best for him, and he should be allowed to express his anger within reasonable bounds.

So how do we deal with a child's anger? Suggest to the thinking child that he read a book on war or watch a violent program on TV, but that he not pull a mean trick. Tell the doing child to throw rocks or snowballs at the fence, not the windows. He has to work out his anger physically, but not on his siblings or classmates.

Thinking people are creative, and inspiration begins by fantasizing, but unless ideas are brought to fruition they are lost to fantasy life. The thinker usually doesn't act them out but explains them to someone with doing abilities, so a creative idea is passed from one thinking person to another, then to a doing person and perhaps another until it is finally acted upon. Each person involved, like a link in a chain, adds, subtracts or changes the idea until the original may be unrecognizable.

"Think tanks" are made up of extreme thinkers, intelligent,

creative, innovative people who come up with new ideas and solutions to problems. They rarely implement their concepts but pass them on to the doers. There are several commercial enterprises of this nature, and thousands of people serve the same purpose individually, both officially and unofficially.

The monks and nuns of the Middle Ages had predominantly thinking personalities. As a rule, they chose this type of life because their extreme thinking tendencies made it difficult for them to cope with the secular world. While they were effective in intellectual and imaginative fields, they were inadequate on the doing side. In monasteries and nunneries they had an organized life in which they could do their work and feel comfortable.

Today there are many people in similar situations. Librarians and accountants and writers are not in contact with people but deal with things or numbers or words or inanimate objects. Many predominant thinkers are attracted to such secluded environments in which to work. They are all part of the scheme of things and the world needs them.

Most thinkers are valuable people. They are dedicated and conscientious—the best kind of employee. However, they can become slaves to work if these tendencies become a compulsion that grows until it is running their lives. We hear of the "workaholic," which is compulsive perfectionism, and should be watched. I fight this when I find myself tidying my desk over and over, detailing every transaction, making notes of unimportant matters. I pick up fluff from the carpet, empty half full scrap baskets and wipe the kitchen counters again and again. Scrupulosity is usurping time from worthwhile work.

The doing side is visible to the world and influences what we do. It is creative and artistic, but in a different way than thinking. It deals more easily with people than with things. It is the element that is extroverted, happy-go-lucky, gregarious and loves excitement and fun. Doing is involved whenever the body moves as the brain communicates with muscles. It is the acting out trait which is essentially living—everything we do, every move we make, everything we say.

The doing side loves activity, moving the body is its dish of tea. The body was created to move, and movement is a stimulant and a relaxer of tense moments. Unwittingly, man devised many forms of motion to appease his body's demands. That is why we have games and sports—baseball, football, hockey, basketball, golf, tennis and dancing, to name a few. Man conceived dancing and music to satisfy his emotional, social and sexual needs, which conform to his body's rhythms, the walk, the heartbeat, the breathing. So the doing side has a plethora of pleasures from which to chose and the thinking side indulges in these to the extent of its needs.

People with more doing than thinking are people oriented, and usually chose a career that involves people, such as selling, directing, or administration. Extreme doers often choose a career that allows them to exert influence over others, such as religion and politics. The artistic person with more doing expresses his talent in doing ways. He is more apt to be a speaker, a musician, an actor or a dancer; the more thinking, a painter, a sculptor, an architect, a playwright or a poet.

Many of those who commit crimes have an excessive amount of the doing element. They don't learn by being jailed and when released, resume the same lifestyle. So the public continues to be threatened by drug addicts, thieves, muggers and murderers. Up until the last fifty years, these criminals were banned from society.

There is a type of personality that has no conscience and is totally immoral. We have become familiar with such human entities through the press. How can a person go into a convenience store, hold up the proprietor, empty the cash register, then shoot him dead? How can the rapist beat up a women, have his way with her, then slash her throat or shoot her? Why is it that these criminals are apprehended, tried and found guilty and sent to prison and many released on parole after serving a minimum term? Then they resume their lifestyles and kill, rape or rob again. And there are the serial killers, the "Son of Sam", the "Hillside Strangler" and Charles Manson who murdered eight people, all for no reason. What motivates these people? Is there a malfunction in their brains that causes this behavior?

We call them psychopaths. The word is not used very often in ordinary conversation. One seldom hears it, however, it is the term for the hardened individual described above who chooses crime as his career, the career criminal. These people are utterly incapable of experiencing the usual emotional sensations we feel, such as compassion, love, understanding, pity, guilt, remorse.

The career criminal has the "gift of gab" and a remarkable facility for talking his way out of scrapes and ingratiating himself to his listener. He uses words of love and endearment with ease, and vents emotions and sympathy, but has no capacity to feel what he is saying. He understands the words and what they mean at the intellectual level but has never and will never be conscious of them. If he is caught in a lie, he quickly changes the subject and shifts into another.

Psychopaths are recognized easily by applying a formula worked out by scientists who have studied them for many years. They all have the same characteristics. Aside from the traits mentioned above, the psychopath is charming and ingratiating. He introduces interesting subjects into the conversation with glibness, and an eloquence that demonstrates more than average intelligence. He can talk himself out of any situation and can fool all but the interrogator who is informed and does not fall for his line.

The psychopath is also found in other fields of endeavor. The professions and business are not exempt from their share of shysters, insider traders, unethical doctors, and dishonest businessmen. The world is full of evil people who pray upon society and cause inestimable hardship to innocent people, but don't take human life.

Studies by scientists for which special tests were devised, show that the psychopath, eighty percent of whom are men, clearly indicate that they have no understanding nor do they experience feelings of emotion or the pangs of conscience, as we do. When they kill, they feel nothing but a sense of accomplishment, a job well done. And as well as being devoid of compassion they are also devoid of fear. Further research clearly indicates that the psychopath has a defect in the brain that points to a failure in its development.

The psychopath is a con man. He is irresponsible and manipulative, a fluent and smooth talker, naive yet selfish, charming, yet callous and an easy and convincing liar. He loves to break the laws laid down by society. He is completely amoral. He lives only in the present and what it can bring him, and has no desire to plan ahead. This shows a state of immaturity which, with age, usually improves. Consequently, it is the opinion of some researchers that there is hope that the psychopath can be rehabilitated through a well designed program of psychotherapy to accelerate his maturation. Up until now, it was believed by all studying the psychopath that there was no hope for treatment and he is destined to be incarcerated for the rest of his life.

At this point in history, the urgency to find the answers to criminal behavior has never been greater. Statistics show that the incidence of psychopaths in the general population is rising steadily, especially within inner cities. Their numbers now are from two to three percent. Furthermore, the crimes are being committed by younger and more brutal individuals. It is well documented that the criminal begins his escapades at home very early in life, and grows up with a history of being in and out of trouble with the law until he is an adult.

What has not been documented for lack of sufficient data is the incidence of individuals in the everyday stream of business and the professions, who disrupt and destroy the well-being, albeit not the lives, of countless of innocent people. Scientists believe that their lack of guilt, empathy and consideration is as great as that of the criminal who rapes, tortures or kills his victim. And not many of these so-called white collar criminals end up in prison. They remain moving about freely in society wreaking havoc, doing harm and profiting thereby, with no retribution.

This brings us to the matter of crime and drugs. Does a criminal on drugs have an impact on the crime he commits? Is someone on drugs who is not a criminal apt to commit a crime? The experts say, yes. Although drugs have always been available to the few who turn to them, the past fifteen years show an insurgence of their use unparalleled in history. We submit that the advent of the form of cocaine called "crack" is the cause of this tremendous increase in crime. The public does not realize what crack does to the workings of the brain. Most users would probably abandon it, if they had the facts.

The drug experience began among young people in the 1960s and twenty years later America became the greatest consumer of illicit drugs in the world, especially the most dangerous, cocaine. The use of cocaine is harmful to the body as well as to the brain. Sudden death from cocaine is not uncommon and can be caused by other hard drugs as well. It is known to damage the heart, causing rupture of heart muscle, it decreases the supply of blood and oxygen to the heart, causing damage to blood vessels in the brain resulting in death. It damages the liver, kidneys and depletes the immune system, laying the body open to disease.

When cocaine is smoked, sniffed or injected it goes immediately to the brain and gives a euphoric feeling. It produces that feeling by traveling straight to the primitive Old Brain, called the "limbic system", which controls drives and emotions and the essential processes for survival, such as nutrition and reproduction. The Old Brain is surrounded by the New Brain, or "neocortex," which is the center of intelligence, reasoning powers and self consciousness. These two brains complement one another and each is necessary to the other.

Cocaine causes the release of an excessive amount of neurotransmitter substances in the brain, namely, norepinephrine and dopamine, which damages the cells of the heart. It also produces compulsive and irrational behavior, and extreme paranoia. The intellect is affected, and the ability to reason, thus removing inhibitions and allowing a free rein to emotions and passions, including anger and violence.

Cocaine interferes with the body's homeostasis, lowering the sense of physical well-being and emotional stability. As yet there is no sure cure for drug abuse of any kind, although much work is being done to find it. Some people are able to drink alcohol moderately and never become alcoholics. Some can take an occasional snort of cocaine or marijuana and not become addicted, but until we find the secret of addiction in the individual, it is best never to experiment with drugs, especially hard drugs. For some of us are born addictive to drugs, to food, to gambling, to work or to whatever turns us on and until we find the answer as to why and how to harness this craving, be careful.

However, not all extreme doers are criminals. We meet people in everyday life who have a tendency to disregard the feelings of others and don't really care if they do. They have no sympathy and ride rough shod over everyone, leaving a trail of unhappiness behind them. They make poor husbands and wives and worse parents, as they have little understanding. They may cheat at cards, drink too much, abuse their spouses, act out sexually, and give the impression of indifference and "couldn't care less." These traits are intensified when combined with a large degree of paranoia, which makes them unscrupulous and greedy, egocentric and demanding. They can be asocial and amoral, and often driven to seek positions of power, in which they thrive, some to do good, some to do evil. Such people tend to gravitate to big business, evangelism and politics, all areas of control.

EVERYONE HAS SOME PARANOIA

Aside from the four cornerstones, all personalities contain other ingredients as well, the most important of which is paranoia. You hear the word often, and conclude it means fear, but there is a great deal more to paranoia. Look it up in the dictionary. You will he surprised that Random House, Funk and Wagnalls, Oxford and Webster describe paranoia as a mental disorder, although its broad concept has been around since before Hippocrates. There is a rare illness call paranoia, but we will define it as the personality trait which we all possess.

Paranoia is an essential element and a quality which every living thing is born with, from the tiniest insect to the complex human being. Even plants and trees have it. It is like a sixth sense and has many facets which color everything we think and do. It is a prerequisite to accomplishment and the driving force that spurs on energy. It is the compulsive, aggrandizing, egotistical, shrewd, controlling side of a personality, and if these characteristics are not in excess, they help us focus on goals, reach them and retain them.

On the one hand, paranoia protects us, warms us, enfolds us and generates courage and self-criticism and causes us to be careful, and cautiously defensive. On the other, it makes us fearful, apprehensive, suspicious, critical, hostile and self-assured. It is the element that brings out gossip and deceit and makes us blame others when things go wrong. Paranoia drives us to control situations and the people around us, and to manipulate them so we can. It is the part of personality that is hard to live with, yet we cannot live without it.

Paranoia has many facets and being afraid of physical harm is one, that apprehensive feeling so necessary to protect us. It is being self-centered, our selfish element. Are you unfriendly at times? Do you stiffen when the doorbell rings? Do you suspect a stranger's motives? All living things, including us, react to fear in a primitive way called the "fight or flight" syndrome. Paranoia wakens this, and when caught in a crisis, we have to decide quickly whether to run away or stay and fight. Wild animals could not survive without paranoia and people react the same as animals when threatened. So paranoia is our constant companion, always ready when needed.

If we have too little, we are trusting to a fault. This makes us defenseless and vulnerable to exploitation and fraud. Friends take advantage of us and use us without regard for our well-being, and families and friends take from us and never give in return. We are open to undeserved criticism, and can be physically hurt because we have little fear. We are naive and unworldly and believe everything we hear, which sometimes leads us into trouble.

Others have too much and excessive paranoia creates grasping, greedy, self-serving individuals, possessed with gaining control over the lives and possessions of others. They ignore all opinions except their own and don't trust anyone. They are constantly afraid of being attacked and always on the offensive without provocation and walk rough shod over those they consider in their way. Their dealings with people can be unpleasant, as they distrust without reason and blame others if something goes wrong—never themselves. They are suspicious without cause and question the kindest motives, and harbor unwarranted anxiety and insecurity. If high energy and an excessive doing personality are added, that person is dangerous.

The only way to get along with an extreme paranoid is to agree with him in everything. Allowing your life to be controlled is the price for peace.

People with high paranoia are socially accepted despite their affinity for sarcastic and biting remarks, but they can be hostile if challenged and are apt to blame others for their mistakes and shortcomings. This is their defense to cover up their insecurity and lack of self-esteem. They are often highly successful and great achievers, but seldom find happiness, especially in close relationships. Control is the primary objective of strongly paranoid people and the world is run by them. Politicians have a lot, as have many religious leaders. Neither would choose these careers were it not for their compulsion to control. We also find the paranoid personality scattered among friends and acquaintances and it is best to be alert when you discover their makeup. Know this quality in yourself as well as in others. The knowledge will assist your appraisal of all people and allow you to understand them.

What is the right amount? Does anyone have a correct percent of paranoia? The right amount can be determined only by each individual, as we all differ in the makeup of our personalities and the interaction of our components with paranoia. Check yourself out and compare yourself to what you consider an ideal person. We, the authors, think we don't have enough and have had to learn to protect ourselves, although we cannot increase the degree with which we were born.

[21]

So paranoia is always around, ubiquitous, with its infiltration into all facets of life. We mentioned the excessive paranoid personality which is best to steer clear of, for these people always hurt us; but if they are close to us, we may deny the pain to continue the relationship. Such a boss does not keep employees long, for he demands total deference to his destructive way of thinking and is unable to respond to anyone's emotional needs. The only employees who stay with him are of the extremely passive type or are so in need of a job they tolerate him. We can identify these personalities by their compulsion to control those around them, although this is sometimes done in such as obtuse fashion it is difficult to detect. The scholarly and artistic types, usually thinkers, confine their efforts largely to the family circle, with unhappy prospects for all. The doing type extends this scope into the community, with results such as the Ku Klux Klan or other extremist groups.

A typical case of the paranoid thinker is Samantha. who is insecure, possessive, and highly dependent on her husband. Morbidly jealous of his family, she wears them down with incessant hostility, one by one. Her criticisms serve to undermine family faith and trust with the ultimate objective of alienating everyone from her husband, who seems oblivious to her machinations. In driving off his relatives, Samantha satisfies her paranoid possessiveness and maintains control over him. Eventually, she succeeded in estranging the members of both his and her families.

Another example is Maryanne, a widow who clings to a grown son for her emotional needs. He feels obliged to remain at home and sublimates his needs in intellectual and athletic pursuits, which never really fulfill him.

And there is Karen, a young woman who consulted a psychiatrist because her father rejected her after his remarriage. The stepmother created an atmosphere so unbearable that Karen left home. Her attempts at conciliation were ignored, and crushing remarks and personal criticisms were thrown at her. Psychotherapy helped her adjust but the situation never improved. The doctor explained that the stepmother has a strong paranoid personality and had "brain washed" the father against his daughter. Karen was advised to stay away from them.

We read in the newspaper of people who died alone in apparent poverty and were found to have fortunes tucked away in the walls of their houses. The Collier brothers were typical. They feared that someone would rob them or they would overspend and become destitute, so they lived as misers. This is a passive type of paranoia, with excessive suspicion and the compulsion to accumulate and hold on to possessions.

Highly creative and power-oriented people have great influence, especially in politics, business, statesmanship and religion. They work their way to the top through high intelligence, energy and paranoia. The politician or clergyman takes a radical or a right wing approach and is a fiery orator. Some change the course of history, for good or ill, with an intense drive to dominate and control the masses. While the paranoid doer is persistent and potentially dangerous, the paranoid thinker sets out to solve problems and do good. However, both demand control over others which interferes with individual freedom.

So extreme paranoia is not always for bad, it can also be for good. Extraordinary thinkers in religious history include Jesus Christ, Gautama Buddha, Mohammed, and other evangelists whose influence has survived the ages. They devoted their lives to pursuits that affect the well-being of millions. Contemporary examples are Winston Churchill, J. Pierpont Morgan, J. Edgar Hoover and Howard Hughes, all of whom contributed enormously to the successful progress of civilization. These all had extreme paranoia.

On the other hand, the Old Testament has several examples of spiritual leadership that can go wrong. Men like King Saul began with great promise, but once they achieved kingship, their manipulative doing side emerged to turn them into tyrants. A modern case is that of Jim Jones of Guyana infamy, who began by doing good and attracted the weak and dependent into a cult that became a suicide/murder pact. Such cases exemplify the danger that lurks not only in the excessively paranoid personality, but in the extreme passivity of the followers who give their leader control.

There are paranoid power plays throughout history. The lust for power is seen from the Roman persecution of the Christians to the Aztec practice of human sacrifice, which the priesthood justified to the necessity of appeasing the gods. The real motive, however, was the need for total control of the people.

Dictatorships are still common in today's world. Even petty bureaucrats show mildly paranoid personalities. Government means control, and the gap between theory and practice is glaringly apparent in officials who take bribes and otherwise abuse their positions. Paranoia also infiltrates the arena of finance, where the powerful forces of greed dominate the doing side. Intentions may be initially honest, but their enactment in the market place can be anything but.

Adolf Hitler was a classic paranoid psychopath. He took advantage of the demoralized state of his country to rise from obscurity to relentless power. It is fortunate for Western civilization that he was opposed by Winston Churchill, one of the master statesmen of all time. Churchill's paranoia was channeled by intelligence and energy to create leadership qualities of a high order.

As of this writing, the entire world is threatened by another paranoid psychopath, Saddam Hussein of Iraq, who is so aptly described by the press as "another Hitler."

Howard Hughes, the corporate empire builder, was extremely paranoid in both business and personal matters. He had an abiding fear of being poisoned and would eat nothing that had not been prepared by a trusted staff member. He also had a deep seated dread of disease and wore gloves to shake hands and touch objects. Drug use worsened these tendencies, and he died a recluse.

Paranoia can be international. Groups and entire nations can be caught up in it. This was seen in the recent state of affairs between the United States and the Western world and the U.S.S.R. The sword of Damocles was nuclear attack, the fear of which incited hostile suspicion and aggressive action. No one knew the real magnitude of the threat, and the unknown is fertile ground for the growth of paranoia, as exemplified by the arms race. This threat has eased and the world has embarked on a dramatic turnabout. We have yet to find out what will emerge and how the crisis in the Middle East will resolve.

THINKING AND DOING WORKING AS A TEAM

Thinking and doing are constantly working together. The balance of the two regulates how we feel and what we accomplish, and shifts rapidly from one to the other. For instance, I am at the typewriter, but my thinking is hard at work, about ninety percent thinking and thirty percent doing. If I didn't type or say what I think no one would know my thoughts, so what we think is never known unless we speak or write it. However, not every act is accompanied by thinking or vice versa. When I brush my teeth my mind may be a blank, and by the same token I may be relaxing not moving a muscle, while my mind is busy solving a problem. However, brain energy is being utilized, so that either thinking or doing causes equal fatigue.

The amount of thinking and doing used together fluctuates, and the percentage of each can reach one hundred, but not at the same time; when one reaches a hundred, the other is lowered. For example, a bank robber uses more thinking while he plans a robbery, but while he is robbing he makes a supreme effort, using 90% of thinking and 90% of doing. When a tennis player reaches the finals at Wimbledon, he uses one hundred percent of doing and seventy-five percent of thinking. This produces an extraordinary burst of energy motivated and controlled by the brain. When the match is over, the balance of thinking and doing returns to its original level.

Thus, the balance between thinking and doing changes according to what is being done. Working at a desk requires more thinking, an athlete uses more doing. Each activity has a different balance but the original balance remains unchanged for life. Thus the doer is usually a better athlete and the thinker more intellectually capable. Great ability in both is rare.

The thinker is rigid, dedicated, sensitive. He likes to use his brain and thrives on detail. The doer enjoys being with people, acting and reacting with them. The contrast is roughly that of the college professor and the salesman. Both make use of people, the former more indirectly, the latter more openly. A high amount of paranoia would push either to an unhealthy degree of control and manipulation.

MANY TALENTS GO TO WASTE

We are born with talents and it is up to us to develop them. There are great athletes who never make it, talented actors who drop out after one success. There are brilliant people who get a Ph.D. and end up painting houses. Aspiring writers are going to write that great novel but fritter away their lives on trivia. Why this waste of talent? Usually, it is because of low or misdirected energy coupled with other factors, such as the lack of inspiration, a doing personality preferring to enjoy life, a tendency to indulge oneself, the unwillingness to work hard, or the abuse of the body by alcohol or drugs. All block the development of talent and stop the flow of capability. Physical handicap is not a deterrent, in fact it often appears to augment ability. So what is accomplished is determined by how a life is managed.

What we plan to achieve may be unrealistic and does not materialize. This applies to many works of art, painting, sculpture, music, literature, architecture. The artist knows what he wants to produce, but is frustrated throughout the process, and even if the final product is proclaimed a masterpiece, he is not satisfied. This holds true for the performing arts as well. A dancer or an actor is constantly seeking perfection and striving to correct the tiny flaws undetectable by the observer. The more thinking person blames himself for falling short of his goal; the more doing tends to excuse himself for turning out a second rate product and may claim that something interfered with his work.

The desire to give and take affection is a powerful need closely linked to thinking and doing. A more doing person is likely to be affectionate in the physical sense, wanting to touch and be touched; the thinker tends to avoid physical contact. It doesn't mean he lacks affection but it is difficult for him to be demonstrative. Doers find this hard to understand, just as thinkers cannot understand the desire for "hands on" love.

The link between the thinking and the doing is not well understood but they work together smoothly most of the time. Thinking is controlled by invisible chemical changes in the brain and doing is expressed in visible activity from electrical impulses. And life has its opposing sides, play and work. There is physical play like tennis and golf, intellectual play, such as chess and bridge, and emotional play, like acting and dancing. There is also addictive play in drinking and drugs.

The work segment of life is also varied. There is physical work as farming, carpentry or in a factory, intellectual work as a scientist or mathematician, and emotional occupations as an actor or musician.

As most of us are one-sided, it is easy to slip into using the dominant side to the neglect of the other. The doer likes to be with people and may let play interfere with work; the thinker is apt to indulge in reading, writing and study, retreating more and more into self. We choose to do whatever fulfills us because it is the strongest side, and we build it up, resulting in reducing the strength of the other. It takes effort to reach the right balance. So managing life is largely a balancing act, like keeping a scale or a seesaw on the level. And aside from thinking and doing and work and play, there is paranoia, and this balance is very delicate, for we have to be able to judge between the valuable part and the dangerous part. So we should work for a balance and not stay lopsided, for an imbalance is a dissatisfied person. The workaholic will burn out and the playaholic will be defeated by excess.

WHAT IS INTELLIGENCE?

It is the capacity for thinking and learning, the ability to understand, to grasp concepts, to reason and to make use of and apply this knowledge. It involves problem solving skills, both mental and physical, and the aptitude to translate thoughts into words. Performance is the best criterion for gauging the degree of intelligence, so to make a fair judgment, one should know a person pretty well. Conversational content is a clue as well as accomplishment in a demanding field, and can be an important factor in a business or profession. High achievement in school speaks well for intellect, however, low marks do not preclude high intelligence, as there are many different types and forms. Intelligence differs from person to person and can be verbal, mathematical, artistic, mechanical, athletic, financial, sexual and others. We are apt to disparage types we lack. The athlete, for example, does not think much of the scholar, and the scholar looks down on the athlete. However, they are equally intelligent in their own fields.

The intelligence quotient—I.Q.—test has been used for decades to measure intelligence, and is still considered the best, although it is only one of many. It determines, however, only verbal and mathematical skills and does not show potential for aesthetic or three-dimensional thinking, athletic and social abilities and so forth. It does not spell out aptitude for writing, playing the piano, or painting, for a great artist or athlete can be as intelligent as a renowned mathematician. There are other tests that can provide a more accurate assessment.

WHAT IS ENERGY — OR DRIVE?

Energy is a force that comes from brain metabolism and is entirely under its control. We also call it "drive." Every living thing is a mechanism that converts its energy into mental and physical activity. We are born with a certain amount of drive that emanates from the brain and directs thinking and doing, as man transforms it into technology indispensable to society. Energy motivates each of us to develop the talents and skills we have in order to achieve our goals in life.

Each bit of life, whether it be a tiny amoeba, a plant, an animal or a human being, starts out with a burst of energy. The sperm uses its bit to search for the egg and implant itself. This is true of pollen carried by a bee, the seed from a tree fluttering to the ground, or the sperm of fish and animals. Once that bit of life finds its niche, it takes in nutrition and turns it into energy, then grows and changes until it has reached its full potential. This is true of all forms of life on earth, animate and inanimate. For example, the goldfinch converts his energy into flight and song, and joins with his mate to produce the next generation of goldfinches.

The earth is also an energy mechanism, acquiring most of it from the sun and converting it into changes on its surface. It is growing and getting hotter as the sun pours energy onto it, creating storms and winds, rains and blizzards, tornados and hurricanes, earthquakes and volcanoes.

A leaf starts as a tiny bud and takes in sunlight, water and food from the tree's roots. It grows and fulfills its mission until the fall, when it shrivels and falls to the ground, to us a waste product, but to nature it is a collection of atoms, the building blocks of matter, which are constantly changing, but always available. Our bodies are made of atoms that may have come from trees that died millions of years ago or rocks that were on the moon, even from solar dust. Our atoms will eventually be a part of some totally unrelated thing, perhaps an elephant or a laurel bush, an airplane or a satellite.

To nature, recycling its atoms, is merely a reshuffling of the infinite numbers of the ever available supply, each having a special purpose in the scheme of things. This interpretation is humbling, the orderly immensity of the plan mindboggling. This is really what life is, and we all are a part of the scheme. What this adds up to is that we are converting mechanisms composed of millions of atoms constantly throwing out energy, each person doing his or her thing in his or her way, never two alike. We are a tiny part of a huge transforming process and perform according to our individual personalities, the thinkers thinking and the doers acting out.

Why don't we stop and do nothing for a change? Because we can't. Our energy has to be used, and some of us move slowly and some fast and some spin their wheels, but none stands still. So the universe is in a state of perpetual motion; the earth keeps turning and living things on its surface race to use the energy they generate, and we are caught up in this restless activity. It is the way it has always been and always will be.

Where do we get this limitless energy? It comes from two sources, inheritance and the food, water, air and sunlight taken into the body, nourishment from inside and out. It is converted into action, thought, emotion, spiritual values and so forth. The amount of energy expended is determined by the degree possessed, which can range from high to moderate to low, influenced by the degree of intelligence. We all differ in the ability to transform energy into achievement, which largely depends on the talents and motivation of the individual.

The level of energy can be affected by changes in mood; if we are depressed the level is down, if up, the sky is the limit. Energy is depleted by poor nutrition, injury, illness and abuse of the body, and outside elements, such as lack of exercise, play a role in regulating it and the persistence of effort. Self-motivated work, as that of a writer or artist, takes a lot of energy. The pace is slower with no outside stimulus, as competition accelerates its production and outflow, utilizing it to the fullest extent.

Some people have limited energy, resulting in low mental and physical drive, and it is unfair to label them lazy, for there are many advantages to this type of personality. They may move slowly, but are more persistent than high energy people, and less hasty in their reactions. They make shrewder and more accurate decisions, because they take time to consider and absorb the facts before acting. They may live longer because they develop lifestyles that are easy going, and hence better balanced, so they are happier than many others. These people live in a quieter, more self-possessed way than do those with high energy, and make comfortable adjustments because they don't drive themselves. They are good company and make satisfying relationships, and accept the fact that they are not world beaters and are not envious of those who are.

The low energy person with high intelligence is not a happy person, because he blames himself for his lack of achievement in life. This creates tension and anxiety as he tries to accomplish what he lacks the energy to do, and moves from one project to another without making progress in any.

The vast majority of the population has moderate energy levels, and steadily weaves its way through life with surprising determination. They are in the professions, in teaching and are the white and blue collar men and women who contribute enormously to business and industry, and carry the bulk of the nation's workload. They are mothers and housewives, and those who choose politics and religion. Many are of high intelligence and represent every sphere of work. They are most of the people we know, and the world needs them.

Those with high energy and high intelligence are the greatest achievers and are always in the public eye. They are presidents of big corporations, prominent politicians, famous doctors and lawyers, renowned artists, men and women in every discipline. They are the jet set who dash through life, projecting ahead and planning projects and changes. The world needs them too, for they promote progress in every field.

And there are high energy people with moderate intelligence. There are housewives and mothers, who expend most of their time on family and home. They are active in community affairs, contributing their talents to the church, the hospital or a charity, and have many projects that improve the home and please the family.

Those in the work force with high energy generally are superior employees, and accomplish more than their colleagues. The exception is the person with low intelligence who is running all the time but gets nowhere. Each, however, has his place in the scheme of things.

So energy is the driving force within us. It determines to a great extent how far a person goes in life. It does not change, and the level can be maintained by preserving health.

THE PACE OF LIFE
Everybody goes through life at a different pace and we instinctively set the rate best suited to us. It seems to have a rhythmic pattern. Some of us go at a tremendous speed, some moderately, and others slowly. This is not fully understood, but we do know that pace is related to energy level, personality, upbringing and habits formed from the environment. For example, compare a butcher and a taxi driver who have the same energy level. The butcher slices and chops with precision, so he sets his pace to a speed he can handle, the taxi driver needs less physical but more mental energy to reach his destination without incident. He seems to be expending more energy than the butcher, but they are both using the same amount.

A person growing up in New York City sets a faster pace than one with the same energy level growing up in Great Falls, Montana, but if he moved to Great Falls, his pace would slow considerably. By the same token, the president of a large American corporation sets a faster pace than the leader of a mountain tribe in Afghanistan, although they may have a similar degree of energy. So the environment has a considerable impact on the amount of energy exerted.

Certain personality traits can influence pace, contrary to the norm. For example, an intense, high energy person may go at things slowly and painstakingly and establish a rhythm that is difficult to alter. This shows an extreme thinking nature out of balance with compulsivity. Setting priorities will result in a more flexible routine and a happier person. Another with high energy may set a fast pace and jump from one project to another without finishing any. This is a sign of impatience and impulsiveness linked to immaturity, and is also related to high mood. That person races through the day, wanting things done yesterday, flipping from person to person, knowing no one really well.

We can control the pace of life but this takes effort and the key is determination to change the way we manage our lives. If we cram too much into one day, we should set priorities, too slow a pace can be speeded up by committing to a daily schedule. If a person is unable to change, it is a sign of rigid right brain thinking.

WE HAVE OTHER CHARACTERISTICS

One is passiveness/aggressiveness. These are opposite forces that stay in the background waiting to be called upon when needed. We have some of each and how we use them depends on the amount we have and the circumstance that arouses them. A more passive person is submissive and unresisting, and does not react to events that stir up emotions. A more aggressive person attacks for little or no reason. These are the extremes and most of us have varying degrees in between. One cannot determine if a person is more passive or more aggressive until a challenge arises. Then the reaction signifies the degree.

We cannot predict how far a person will go when provoked. An insult may be taken lying down or by an explosion of protest and this can happen to a normally passive person, when really incensed. Conversely, an aggressive person may react to an attack with passivity if sufficiently intimidated. So both can react in an uncharacteristic manner. Aggressive people are skillful at manipulating others, while passive people tend to be self-effacing and less obviously a threat, but this can also be an effective manipulation. To take the equivocal, "on the fence" approach to life is a sign of passivity, and a determined, strong willed attitude that is a little pushy shows aggressiveness. The passive person lets others make decisions, the aggressive voices his opinions in an assured fashion.

If a person barges in on a conversation and presses his point, he is aggressive. If he sits back and waits for others to speak, he is taking the passive role. As he has both potential qualities, experience may prompt him to restrain his aggressive side and call on the passive. The opposite is also true. The overt aggressor is an irritant, but the passive aggressor can score just as many points.

Obsessive compulsiveness is another trait. This is our "fussy" quality and shows up at an early age. Some babies can't stand to have wet faces, cry until their mothers wipe them and scream until their diapers are changed. Other babies are not bothered by wet faces or dirty diapers and go happily to sleep, totally oblivious.

If this trait is strong we keep tidying up around the house and at work, and when something is out of place, we are uncomfortable until we put it where it belongs. We are meticulous about appearances, and disorder is distressing to us. Those who have little are untidy about their persons and belongings and unconcerned if the house or office is in shambles. They don't care what others think and can be comfortable in disorder. Most of us fall in between these extremes.

Some people are so compulsive that they pick up every thread and tidy the house over and over. Some brush their teeth or wash their hands repeatedly, or carry out some pointless activity again and again. This is the extreme form of obsessive compulsiveness and, when it interferes with one's life, is neurotic. An outside challenge goes a long way toward expending the energy used in this needless behavior.

So this is our meticulous, finicky feature, and is colored as always by thinking and doing. Let's compare Sheila and John. Sheila is compulsive about keeping the house in order and her appearance impeccable. She always looks as though she came out of a bandbox. John tends to be untidy in his dress and surroundings. However, if Sheila insists and the occasion requires him to be well-groomed, he can pull himself together and present a commendable image, which shows that he has considerable compulsiveness in his makeup, but his doing side overrides it most of the time.

There are couples who are poles apart in this respect, for example, the husband is a tidy person, the wife terribly sloppy. For them, communication is the key to peaceful living, so talking about it and playing a little game can ease the tension. The game is to switch roles, and it can be fun! Neatnik John leaves his clothes in a heap, the cap off the toothpaste and the dishes in the sink. Sheila hangs up her clothes, puts her shoes away and makes the bed. After a day or so the atmosphere is lighter and both find themselves laughing at each other's attempts to change. They are relaxed and ready to work out a compromise. This stratagem can be applied to any situation where people are living or working together.

Scientific studies prove that qualities such as these do not change and cannot be forcibly changed. For example, if a man is born honest, he is honest as a child, a teenager and an adult. If born dishonest he lies and cheats at the age of five and steals at ten or fifteen. All through life he does what he wants without regard for others, and the need to get his way may drive him to serious crimes. This is the extreme, and not typical of the population, although the environment also has an influence. All these qualities are under the control of the chemical and electrical makeup of the brain, which is set at birth and subject to change only by enormous stress or determination.

We inherit half our genes from our father and half from our mother, including our many ancestors. Our genes give us body build and how we walk and talk. They give us self-confidence or low self-esteem, and whether we are talkative or let others chatter away. They give us speech, body language and the way we act, and all this along with influences of the environment gives clues to our personalities and how we come across to others.

Faces are distinctive and serve as identification. They change as character is built into them over the years but, despite sagging and a few lines, they remain identifiably similar as in early adulthood.

How a person stands and moves is mostly inherited but some idiosyncrasies are learned. We may imitate a mannerism we admire or a way of moving from training as an athlete or dancer. The walk of the cowboy is the result of many hours in the saddle and considered a "macho" image, so a man may cultivate it. A woman puts on airs to appear feminine, and the pitch of voice and manner of speaking add to the impression. These affectations become ingrained and reveal a desire for self-confidence and freedom from anxiety.

Most people, as they reach their thirties, become more self-assured, and this is obvious by the lives they lead. Is it success in business, a profession, homemaking? Or are they low key people with no evidence of achievement? Most fall between these extremes. We can create the image we want, but first must decide what we like that to be. Does a woman want to look glamorous or like the athlete she aspires to be? Does she have aspiration in the business world or is she satisfied with her homemaker role? There are many images to choose from and one that gives self-confidence is right for her.

BUILD YOUR SELF-IMAGE

This is the story of a young woman who shaped her self-image to her liking. "I was eighteen when I became aware that I didn't like the way I looked. I wanted to be glamorous, slim and pretty and was none of these. I was overweight, had a pimply face, a big nose, large hands and feet and wore glasses. Odgen Nash convinced me that "Men never make passes at girls who wear glasses!" What to do? I was working on Wall Street and determined to mold my image to my liking. I went to Elizabeth Arden's and learned how to use makeup, and to the hairdresser for a becoming hairdo. I bought dresses with the help of a friend and found that I could get along without glasses most of the time. I lost forty pounds through self-discipline and learned to accentuate my good features and live with those I could not change. Then I looked in the mirror and was happier about what I saw. I could now hold my head high and my efforts paid off, for soon I was dating frequently, my business career was successful and at twenty-two I married the man I fell in love with."

Self-image is important because it triggers a feedback that affects what others think of us. When we act naturally, we present a positive impression, for the phony doesn't fool anyone. So, if we know how we appear to others, we can relax and be ourselves, and once we feel comfortable with friends and family, we can apply it to strangers. So image is important. It can be changed according to circumstances and is fun, giving spice to what otherwise might be a dull day. We dress for different occasions, and when dressing for the day, plan accordingly. So how we dress sets the mood and the image we want to present, and building a strong self-image allows us to be at ease in any situation and free from the pressures of playing a part.

Is self-image related to selfishness? Are we all basically selfish? A long time ago, an English philosopher claimed that we are, and that "self" dominates all people, and today some social scientists accept this belief. However, controversy abounds. Today most psychologists agree with Freud's ego theory. Those who are nurture oriented and don't believe in hereditary factors, claim that teaching generosity and altruism can do the trick and turn the tide of selfishness.

Another school challenges these beliefs as theories only, and argues that more recent studies strongly suggest that empathy is more prominent a sentiment than selfishness. But the debate goes on with the statement that empathy is "a fragile flower, easily crushed by self-concern," and that no one would exchange places with the afflicted in order to relieve their suffering.

Another study concludes that human nature is basically social rather than selfish. This is based on anthropological findings indicating that people formed groups that competed with neighboring groups for survival, and the sense of belonging is stronger than the most intense selfish motivation. Yet another study holds that the satisfaction of being a "do-gooder" is paramount to the concern for self and sponsored by our increasing intelligence through evolution. Will we ever know the real answer?

2

HOW DOES THE BRAIN WORK?

Whatisthebrain doing when we think? We know what it says, but we can't see or feel it working. It records knowledge we are taught and learn from life experience, which is stored away in memory and can be retrieved, some easily and some requiring concentrated searching, but little is lost beyond recall. The brain has been compared to a supercomputer, but remarkable as a computer is, the brain is far more efficient. A computer can't create nor can it change its programming. The brain can, and can also put together data it receives and come up with innovative conclusions, act on them and end up with new approaches. A computer can't do this. Our world has advanced to where it is today, from a primitive culture to one of high sophistication through the use of our brains.

The brain is made of delicate tissue. It controls everything we do and think, is protected by the bones of the skull and extends at the back of the neck down the spine to its tip. This part is called the spinal cord and is encased by the bones of the back. It controls the muscles in the body that make us move, walk, talk, and breathe. It receives messages from the brain and relays them to the muscles. The brain also receives messages from the muscles, like "Hey, I'm tired, you are making me work too hard!" or "That is too heavy".

The brain has a memory bank with voluntary recall, and when we see, feel, smell, touch and talk, it registers the messages coming from these senses. It thinks, remembers, and controls when and how we move. It also controls the digestive system, the heartbeat, sleep, and the body's other organs. Some authorities say we use only ten percent of its tremendous capacity to think, reason and create.

We can take a picture of the brain with an electro-encephalo-graph, but this shows only electrical activity which is created by a chemical process within the cells whereby positive and negative charges move across cell membrane barriers through the exchange of chemicals via tiny channels. No one knows how we control mental and physical activity, but it is clear that many different electrical and chemical episodes are involved. When the brain tells the muscles in the body to move, electrical activity does it. When electricity moves between the cells to accomplish this, certain chemi-cal changes take place. When we think, or the body moves, both kinds of changes occur and set up an interchange between them, which often results in an imbalance, and it is this constantly recur-ring imbalance that causes battles within the brain.

We can take a picture with the MRI machine, (magnetic reso-nance imaging), but unless the brain is damaged by disease or injury, it will show no change. Why? Because the brain operates on the atomic level, which is invisible with present day technology. The atoms and molecules in the axons and dendrites are flowing in electrical currents and chemical interaction. The neurotransmitters are exchanging messages. However, this is all taking place at an unbelievably rapid rate, while we are asleep as well as awake, much of it without direction or control.

This remarkable brain, how did it get this way? Evolution is the answer. An animal can protect itself and its children and provide food and shelter, but rather than using our minds merely for self-protection, hunting for food, looking for sex and finding shelter, we developed an ability to correlate material, imagine content, and differentiate between self-aggrandizement and progressive achievement. Then we went beyond that to develop a society, relationships, build a culture, create art and literature. We became in fact a developing creature, very different from the primitive ape we came from, although there are still primitive instincts within us, some good, some bad.

So the quality of our thinking changed as we learned, rose to a higher level and consistently moved higher. We don't stop with a momentous achievement, but pass it on to the next generation to develop further. Thus, we are constantly growing and changing, enmeshed in a thinking/doing combination with the capability to deal with the environment in a way that promotes self-interest. And the intelligence grew with us and we became the human beings we are today, half mostly thinking and half mostly doing.

So how does the brain work? We know a good deal about how it does, but by no means all. Research adds new information to the old theories, enhancing some and eliminating others. We know about the brain's chemical and electrical systems and which chemicals cause depression, and we know how to change the unhealthy chemicals to healthy. We know a good deal but how can we find out what actually goes on? We have identified the areas we see with, hear with, smell and taste with, and the sections with which we think different thoughts. We know where feelings are located, anger, love, hate, sympathy, the sex drive and so forth. But none of this is visible while it is happening.

We can identify areas of the brain that control movement and sensation, and the centers for speech, appetite the five senses and intellect. But we don't know where the four cornerstones of personality are located—thinking, doing, energy and intelligence—Or how they interrelate and influence one another. The fact that they do, however, is quite clear. For example, suddenly you smell gas. Your mind sends a message to your body to move toward the source, the kitchen. Your body reacts and interacts in a matter of seconds, directed by the brain. You find the leak and turn it off. This involves three senses—smell, sight and touch. Do they work with one another singly, in pairs or all together? Are they connected in some way, or do they act separately, coinciding with one another at the right split second? Some day research will reveal the answers.

We have the ability to maintain an optimal mental and physical environment, but we do not understand the laws and balancing mechanisms by which we control this. When we are hungry, we eat, when tired, sleep; when we feel stiff, we exercise. To satisfy our sexual appetite, we seek companionship, for intellectual stimulation, engage in interesting work or reach out for entertainment. When we are happy, we laugh. Why? The natural laws that are built into brain cells control these actions. We also have a mechanism that balances thinking and lets us shift from the use of the right brain to the left at will. Another unknown element lets us strengthen the weaker side of personality—whether the doing or the thinking. These mechanisms help us find and maintain the ideal environment.

RIGHT AND LEFT BRAIN THINKING

Our reasoning is done with the right and the left brains. We think with the right very differently than with the left. They don't work together, thoughts switch quickly back and forth. We don't feel anything when they do, but we can tell which side we are using by the content of the thought and can become familiar with the difference through practice. Right brain thinking is inflexible and slow to change, however, it can change. Ideals, morals and religious and political opinions are molded into it during the young years, as principles are formed and integrated into thoughts and acts. As we mature and learn, the right brain fills in the gaps and holds them fast, largely unchanged through life.

The right brain conceives imaginative, artistic and philosophical thoughts, and is the seat of honesty, loyalty, integrity and reliability. It also harbors emotional qualities, such as love of family and. friends, empathy and grief. Romantic love, that elusive but unchangeable quality which inspires people of all ages, rests also in the right brain.

We inherit a capacity to form opinions to fit in with our personalities which come from instruction, the environment and experience, and store them in the right brain. Intuition is another right brain function which gives us insight and provides on-the-spot decisions. Intuitive answers are not always complete or correct, but they can be useful when a snap judgment is needed.

Fantasizing, or daydreaming, is another aspect of the right brain that is satisfying and rewarding. Although unrealistic, daydreams are conceived from unfulfilled desires, and eliminate obstacles, giving the feeling that they are being realized. They relax us and drive out disturbing thoughts, and act as safety valves, giving a partial release to aspirations. Fantasies lift the mood on bad days, as does thinking of something amusing or pleasant. Then spirits rise and can cause a shift from negative to positive thinking. They can also play a part in making decisions by helping us see all sides of a question. Don't smother them, let them blossom.

Daydreaming can enrich boredom like a wait in the doctor's office or a long ride in a car. Fantasy relieves tension and allows the blood to bring oxygen to the brain, furthering its work. For example, exercising with negative thoughts doesn't give the same benefit as with a high mood. Scientific research has proved that angry and negative thoughts are detrimental in that they interfere with the flow of blood to the heart, increase its rate and cause tension.

Daydreaming can improve a skill through imaginary practice. A musician can review a piece in his mind or a singer a song and find his performance improved. The artist visualizes the picture he will paint and his work will go more smoothly. It is the same with sports or any ability that needs perfecting. A dancer can practice a new step mentally with excellent results.

So we are more or less right brain minded and, depending upon the amount of paranoia in our makeup, can be selfish, hostile, suspicious and fearful. However, regardless of these variations, we have fixed ideas and it takes a concerted effort to change them, no matter how open minded we may be.

Conversely, criminal tendencies also originate in the right brain of those with low morality. The antisocial, amoral, criminal mind is not subject to reform, nor does it change through life.

The left brain is flexible and processes exact thinking, such as mathematics and other mind taxing work. It has the reasoning power to organize routine and is extraordinarily adaptable. Unlike the right brain, its thinking develops and changes as we grow in knowledge and experience. Using the left brain is tantamount to having an "open mind". As we grow older, we make less effort to use it and are apt to become more fixed in our opinions. It is a good idea to be aware of this and fend it off, for some people are unable to adjust to changing times as they age.

People whose left brain dominates the right usually choose an exact science as their work, such as business, engineering, accounting, science or mathematics. These require the logic of left brain thinking. Control by the right brain is strongest in the concepts of religion, sexuality, politics and art, but if it has too much leeway, it may be suppressing the left brain's reasoning powers and a person could become a fanatic or a faddist. Deep beliefs in these areas can be altered only by conscious left brain activity and a concerted effort to balance right and left brain thinking. Opinions, however, can be changed from right to left and vice versa.

Ideas about sexuality are usually fixed fairly solidly but can be changed by outside pressures with the help of left brain thinking. Similarly, political convictions, welded into the right brain at an impressionable age can be modified as we grow older. Rigid right brain thinkers can be successful on many levels, but they may also impede progress because of their resistance to change. Social balance requires input from left brain people who act as initiators.

How can we tell which brain is dominant? By our innermost thoughts. Are you usually opposed to the ideas of others? How often do you change your opinion on current issues? Can you change? Do you learn from others, or are you adamant in your beliefs? If your right brain dominates, your answer to these questions is "yes". Are you changeable and easily led? Do you find yourself believing and echoing the last person you talked to? Do you shift from one decision to another only for the sake of pleasing someone? This is left brain thinking.

So the free use of both sides of the brain is essential to a well-rounded personality. It's not easy to achieve this, but knowing ourselves can help build up the weaker side, and reduce the stronger side's domination.

So the right and left brains are often at odds, the right brain more compatible with thinking and the left with doing. The key is to balance the overall use of both, and whether or not to work for this is controversial. As a thinking person with a dominant right brain is better off by exerting left brain influence, and a doing person with a dominant left brain goes to extremes without right brain intervention, the consensus to date is for each of us to make this decision with a thorough understanding of what is involved as far as personal life is concerned.

Human beings have a versatile capability to communicate, but we don't have the ability to coordinate our thinking and doing so they are compatible. Consequently, they clash and battles within the brain result. These are caused by thoughts and ideas that collide, and colliding causes indecision, which is distressing. In addition, male and female qualities and other influences have a way of entering the picture to further complicate things and paranoia is ever present to interfere with clear thinking. Also involved is what we learned from parents and family, religious training, social mores and pressures from friends. So with thinking and doing struggling to overrule one another, a battle within the brain is extremely uncomfortable and at times we wonder what is going on in our heads.

We can usually solve our problems by making decisions but when a conflict arises we are caught in a bind. Why? Because the electrical and chemical substances in brain cells are at cross purposes and we are torn between them and will not be able to function constructively until the chemistry settles down and the balance is restored. What should we do? A change of pace is what we need. Turn on the television, take a brisk walk, read a "who dunnit", confide in a trusted friend. Anything that takes the mind off the problem will cause the chemistry in the brain to regain its balance.

One of the authors learned to cope this way: "When I have a problem, large or small, I ask myself. What can I do about it right now? I usually find something I can do, whether it is a telephone call or a decision to make. Then, I put the problem to one side and go about my business. When I find that I can do something more, I do it, and put it aside again. This goes on until the problem is resolved or works itself out. In the meantime, I can function, although always aware of an unfinished concern."

Thinkers and doers manage life in different ways. For instance, we start the day and find by evening that we didn't accomplish all we had planned. How do we feel? The thinker is frustrated and filled with guilt; the doer doesn't give a damn. But these are the extremes and most of us rationalize that we bit off more than we could chew and will plan differently next time.

Doing people feel trapped in rigid schedules, whether or not self-imposed. They like to feel free to do what they want when they want to. However, they are weak at organizing and function best in a regulated setting. Thinking people are more comfortable in a structured milieu because they are self-disciplined. However, they are inclined to be workaholics, so it's a good idea for them to knock off occasionally and indulge in something on the spur of the moment. They need a change for relaxation. Furthermore, the high energy thinker tends to set up a schedule so full he can't possibly handle it. Only the most rigidly self-disciplined escapes, but does he have much fun in life? It's healthy and human to goof off once in a while.

PLEASURE AND PAIN

Of all the sensations and emotions we experience in life, those that we remember the most are pleasure and pain. Years of observation teaches that the human mind does not enjoy more pleasure or endure more pain than it can handle, and the intensity of pleasure is matched by the intensity of pain. In other words, we never feel one more acutely than the other. Therefore, there is a built in code ingrained in us, as yet undeciphered, that compels us to seek out pleasure and to strive for achievement, which is a form of pleasure. As we reach the pinnacle of success, we bask in the pleasure of fulfillment. When we fall short of our goals, the degree of disappointment is equal to the pleasure.

A pendulum swings from side to side for equal distances. Some have short swings, some medium and some wide. Compare the swinging to the degrees of pleasure and of pain, from high to average to low. This analogy can also be applied to success and failure or to accomplishment and non-accomplishment, always measured by the capacity of the individual relative to the person as a whole and the makeup of his personality.

When a person is born healthy and strong into a family capable of providing the best in life, his capacity for pleasure is enhanced and his potential for pain is also. When a person is born retarded, his pleasures are limited but so is his pain. People who are born complainers also have pleasure, but in their own way, even though they don't seem to be enjoying life. They experience pain as well, but Only to the extent of the pleasure they derive from griping and fault finding. So the individual differences range widely, from very high to very low, and even though someone is always depressed, whose spirits are never up, that person will experience pleasure within his range. So there appears to be a balance in this aspect of life and, as in all human characteristics, it is inherited.

We believe that there is a central meaning to all of life, that it is a common bond between human beings, and that life makes sense. Each of us experiences life in a different context, depending on circumstances, the environment and personality. When you look at a person for whom you are sorry, and say: "Poor thing, I am so lucky", your pity is wasted, for he is operating within his limits and feels a range of emotions as you do. Just as a healthy body is in balance, life is also. No one goes through it in utter misery or in a state of euphoric pleasure. Some people are born with a crippling disease or blind or deaf. Yet their pendulums swing to the happiness and pleasure side as well as to that of despair and pain. There is always a balance.

Is this code regulated? We don't know. Nor do we know why the unfortunate don't suffer more than they do, and when someone is born into riches and is successful, happy and healthy as well, why does he encounter distress and misery? Because the pendulum has to swing back. That is a law of nature and similar to the laws of physics. So, when you see a person to whom your pity flows, don't say: "There by the grace of God go I", for that person may be quite happy in his unhappiness. At this point we get caught up in the identification with our own fantasy of that person's feelings which are quite different from what he actually feels. And the secret is to accept this balance in all things, to understand it and to know yourself well enough to head in a positive direction.

Is this how we should handle the misery that surrounds us? Yes, for how else can a compassionate person survive? He would be emotionally overcome by the miseries of the world and his endurance stretched to the point of breaking. It is fortunate that we suffer the pain only to the extent that we enjoy the pleasure.

The author gives a personal view. "My pleasure is in the accomplishment of whatever task needs doing, large or small, in solving problems, in exchanging communications with someone whose mind I respect and in using my body in an activity, such as tennis, dancing or walking vigorously. These are my pleasures. Aside from physical pain from disease or injury, my pain is psychological, and is derived from the loss of a dear one or a friend, of being hurt by someone near to me, the suffering of someone dear and of individuals throughout the world. Minor pain is derived from frustration in not being able to accomplish my goals."

3

MORE ABOUT PERSONALITY

There are several additional facets to personality. Some we are born with and some not, some can be acquired and some cannot, and there are those we learn voluntarily, either through effort or specific application. Others we acquire automatically through repetition. Some are good and should be kept, others are bad and should be rejected.

Then there are the talents and skills with which we are endowed at birth, waiting to be developed and put to one side until we have the inclination to allow them to mature. We are blessed with many and may channel all our energy into one, the choice depending on the makeup of our personalities. Some of us may perfect a talent or two simultaneously or one after the other, even experimenting with four, five or more over a period of years, successful in some, a failure in others. Some of us may wonder what to do with those we have or are unaware that we have them, so they lie dormant. These natural gifts, however, can be picked up and perfected at any stage in life and turned into a new career or a hobby. Whether or not we use them depends on the individual's level of energy and life circumstances.

Geniuses and those with extraordinary talent are primarily one-sided thinkers and put emphasis on developing their talents to the detriment of their personal lives. Should a gifted pianist attempt to balance the use of his right and left brain? Would his ability suffer? Probably, yes. Such people are extremely successful, but their personal lives are chaotic and most have unhappy childhoods. They often fail in school, don't get along with their peers and nothing goes right until they zero in and concentrate on the talent they have chosen. Then they are off and running, the creative side propelling them into an exciting career. They lack the ability, however, to cultivate gratifying relationships, which would improve with concentration on a balance of left and right brain function, but probably at a price in terms of creativity.

Among the other facets of personality are instincts and habits. Superficially, these appear to be alike. Professionals disagree on the difference between them and some reject the view that human beings, like animals, have instincts. We believe that we do have instincts and that they are inherited. We also feel that we form habits which are motivated by the environment. Scientific research supports this view, however, and both are closely liked to basic personality traits.

WHAT IS AN INSTINCT?

An instinct is a natural aptitude, such as right and left handedness, a sense of direction or sexual interest. Instincts are inherited from our ancestors and stay with us through life. They can be enriched by learning and practice. Those we don't inherit cannot be acquired or learned. We have them or we don't, although manipulative or sly individuals can fake them.

Instincts are primitive and man recoils at being told he is acting instinctively, as his brain has outstripped much that is instinctive by intelligence through evolution. For example, the bird builds its nest by instinct while man resorts to a blueprint, but he still has a strong attachment to home, so the nesting instinct remains. Men have been communicating for thousands of years, first through the senses, then speech and now by sophisticated electronic means. Birds communicate by sound and display, which is sufficient to their needs, so they don't change.

There are two types of instincts, those related to thinking and those to doing. Many resemble those of animals such as nurturing, nesting, mating, homing, and a sense of direction. These are doing functions and common to both humans and animals, but so far as we know, animals do not have thinking instincts which seem to belong to the more sophisticated brain.

The old saying "they cannot see the forest for the trees" is a thinking instinct. It means that some people can only take in the details of a situation but cannot see it as a whole, while others grasp the total picture but overlook the details. There are rare individuals who are able to conceptualize both.

Another thinking instinct is having a closed mind, which is the unwillingness to change an opinion and is traceable to right brain thinking and can override the ability to call on the left brain and be flexible. The emotional basis of deeply held convictions is hard to dislodge, especially those on religion and politics. These become more fixed as we grow older and paranoia becomes more pronounced. As a rule, changes are come by only through a traumatic experience, or through great effort.

Vision is a valuable instinct and few people have it. Those who do are ahead of the times, reaching toward tomorrow. They can conceptualize projects for development in the future and anticipate what others will be thinking and doing decades from now, which often invites derision from those whose view is limited. Leonardo da Vinci was a man of extreme vision, and described aircraft long before they were created by man.

Many people inherit a curious mind. They want to know the "whys" and "hows" of everything, from idle gossip to what makes the leaves change color and how the sea turtle knows where to lay her eggs. People have varying degrees of this instinct, those with the highest often become scientists.

Everyone has incestuous thoughts at times, but they are immediately repelled by instinct, which is nature's defense against inbreeding. When it is ignored, as it was in the time of the Romans, a line degenerates and dies out.

Some people are born with a sense of direction which is a doing instinct. No matter where they are they know the points of the compass. This sense takes them to unfamiliar places and enables them to find their way there again without trouble. Many people don't have this sense and get around by means of route numbers, street names and detailed instructions, but even so they may often get lost.

Right and left handedness is a doing instinct, and early in life an infant indicates an inclination toward one or the other. The eye and the foot usually follow the lead, but some people have a cross dominant eye or foot, meaning that although they are right handed, the left eye or foot is dominant. Lefties make up about ten percent of the population and some people are ambidextrous and have the ability to use either hand with ease.

Most women and some men have the nesting instinct, which to humans is the impulse to create a home. This is most evident in the spring time activity of birds as they gather nest building materials. This instinct is strong in animals and enables them to find a safe place to rest and sleep, and bear and bring up their young. In domestic animals, the dog chooses a special place to lie down, rotating in the area several times. He is following an instinct to smooth his bedding even though it is not necessary.

How does a dove return to the dovecote miles away or a sea turtle know when the tide is at its highest so she can lay her eggs above the waterline? This is the homing instinct and is shared by human beings. What makes us want to be home at night, or glad to be back after a vacation? Why the expression "There's no place like home?" Why are the holidays never the same when spent away from home? At social gatherings, it is interesting to note that women particularly, having chosen a place to sit, invariably return to that same spot. Men tend to be more mobile, but the homing instinct in women shows up in their daily lives.

The territorial instinct is strong, as animals fight to keep the space they have staked out as their own. Man considers his home his castle. It is the last possession he will give up and one of the first he wants to own. Aggression in defense of land extends to nations, as they continually engage in warfare about territorial rights.

Keeping articles of little value is hoarding. It is an instinct and a harmless form of compulsiveness that many people have. We save pieces of string and wrapping paper and find it distressful to give away clothes we seldom wear. It is related to the instinct of some animals to hoard food in the fall to tide them over until spring.

The mating instinct is strong in all life, and the sexual drive is instinctive in humans and in animals, and none need learn how to have sexual intercourse. The first time we make love, we know what to do. No one had to teach us, although it can be further expressed in many ways that are learned. It begins, in both woman and man, with desire, than a physical feeling, which is the thrust of the drive, followed by a primitive impulse, interwoven with the emotional and physical need for sexual satisfaction. The man has an erection spontaneously, producing a need for release. He knows how to proceed and the woman knows how to receive him.

When a young child is allowed to feed himself, he chooses certain foods and rejects others. An inherited instinct guides him. If sweets are offered, he gravitates toward them, but if these are withheld, he will eat the foods his body requires. Most adults, however, are conditioned by family custom and social trends, and their instinct for the right foods becomes adulterated. Children and adults alike have an almost universal affinity for sweets, and it is speculated that this derives from mother's milk, which has a sweet taste.

Although everyone has taste buds, we differ markedly in our food preferences. This same variation applies to everything in life. What one likes another doesn't and there seems to be as much discrepancy in families as in those not related. The genetic variances are enormous. An example is these two brothers. One loves to suck on a lemon and eat sour pickles. The other cannot tolerate lemons or pickles in any form. The very thought makes him pucker up. Some people thrive on spicy foods, to others they are shear agony.

When small children refuse a food that is offered, it is not because they are being ornery, but because it does not taste good to them. The taste for some foods are acquired and it takes growing up before they can be appreciated. Our bodies tell us what is best for us, how much salt to use, water to drink and foods to eat, and what is right for one person may not be for another. We should trust our sense of value in most instances, except for addictive substances which have an undue influence on most individuals.

The tendency to become addicted is an instinct that some people inherit. Cocaine, heroin and other hard drugs, alcohol, nicotine and caffeine are all addictive substances, and chronic overeating is a compulsive activity. You can become addicted without this predisposing instinct, but such addiction is easier to break.

The maternal instinct is observable in most women in varying degrees. It is a thinking/doing instinct and is also present in men, but to a lesser extent. In animals and other forms of life, nurturing ceases once the young are mature enough to fend for themselves, but women experience the desire to mother through life, not only toward their children, but toward those in need.

Altruism, which is closely linked to the nurturing instinct, is unselfish concern for others, especially those in mental or physical distress. When the altruist sees a need, emotional or monetary, he tries to fulfill it. The more thinking person is reticent about this, the more doing inclined to display it.

This is a strong drive in many people, both men and women, and often shows up in the choice of a vocation, like teaching, health care, social work, and other service fields. Altruism also appears in voluntarism, which has long been a hallmark of this country, from the nurse's aide to the volunteer fireman. In daily life, it is seen whenever people go out of their way to help. The Good Samaritan is the classic example.

It is instinctive to be protective of our children and to teach them rules and habits of safety. This applies to us as well, and each person differs in the degree he possesses, varying from the extreme high to the extreme low.

There are many dangers we encounter during a lifetime and it takes years to learn what they are. There is electricity, lightning, deep water, falling, fire and objects that burn or hurt, such as stoves, hot water and knives.

For some it is easy to learn safety habits, for others it is not, so they have to learn the "hard way." They don't listen to others.

WHAT IS A HABIT?

A habit is learned and developed through practice, like tying shoe laces or brushing teeth. A habit becomes automatic and we never think about it unless we make a mistake and have to do it over. When teaching a youngster how to perform what to us is a simple task, it takes a concentrated effort on his part.

The difference between instincts and habits is that instincts are inherited, habits are learned. For example, we are not aware, when driving to work, how we started the car or what our hands and feet are doing. Do we drive by instinct? No, we had to practice until actions became patterns in the brain, programmed into circuits that we call upon and do automatically. We had to learn how to drive and it became a habit. Instincts are inborn, already patterns in our brains.

Sometimes the patterns we learn are not mechanically perfect; they break down and we have to adjust them and sometimes relearn them. Beginning to type again after several years is an example. The pattern is still in the brain but mistakes are made. The habit has to be re-learned. It is the same with any habit such as skating, swimming, shuffling cards, playing tennis, even walking. After it remains fallow for a time, we have to brush up on it. But a habit once learned is never completely forgotten.

Emotions also form patterns and can also be programmed. When we fall in love, we are very conscious of it. We work at it, and the love grows until it becomes well established. Ultimately, it gets to be a habit, and we may neglect to work at it until it is challenged, someone else attracts or the love object is taken away. Then we have to rebuild it and work at understanding it better. Thus, love is like liberty, both require eternal vigilance to preserve it. We will always make mistakes and usually some good comes from them. This is all part of learning and we never stop learning. Mistakes can be incidental or of consequence, and all cause frustration, which is a built in involuntary system that infringes on needs and desires, blocking satisfaction. The thinker is irritated because something interferes with his work and the doer because it interferes with his play. So mistakes are not always valuable, because frustration is so powerful that it pushes everything else aside and holds us back. Then it is time to drop everything and check the balance, for there's a good chance that the less dominant quality has been neglected and needs building up.

Why is life at times so distressing? Because distress is part of the human condition and no one is free from it. It is not destructive, and can be put to good use in order to learn how to balance thinking and doing. This takes effort and practice, as they must be synchronized with life around us, but restoring balance always results in settling the battles in the brain which are causing the distress.

Drives and needs are always with us, competing with one another, emotional, intellectual, physical, spiritual and sexual. While they are persistent, some are desires, not necessities. As each critical point arises, we debate. Is it a necessity or a desire? Should we submit to a desire or only a necessity? We evaluate the pros and cons, establish priorities, come to a conclusion and make a decision.

TALENTS AND SKILLS, IS THERE A DIFFERENCE?

Let us review talents and skills. We are endowed with talents which we are either born with or not, and those we have we must study and practice in order to develop them and become proficient. A skill must also be studied and practiced. So what is the difference if it takes the same effort? Talents are inherited and we cannot acquire them no matter how hard we try or how great is our desire to do so. A skill can be learned and nurtured by anyone and developed into a masterful trade or profession, provided there is the will, the energy and the persistence to perfect it.

A talent is inborn and carries with it the ability to create. Some people have talents which relate to a skill, such as a trade or profession. This could be carpentry, architecture, science, medicine, engineering, all fields in which creative talent can blossom. And talents take many forms, painting, drawing, singing, acting, and playing musical instruments, piano, violin and so forth. These are aesthetic talents. Then there are abstract talents, which apply to business, such as management, marketing and organizational capabilities. Talent extends also into the realm of athletics and the dance. Those who are born with talent can reach the heights of their chosen field, while others who aspire to excel and work very hard, never can. Talents for social manipulation, or for fighting or gambling, cheating or stealing are less attractive but do exist.

Talents run in families but not always from one generation to the next. Sometimes a generation or two is skipped or a talent suddenly appears, hitherto unknown in the family. For instance, my mother and grandmother were creative artists. My two brothers and I inherited none of this, but my daughter and one of my five sons did. So you never know when a talent is going to pop up or not appear at all.

Anyone can develop a skill and we all learn many in the course of daily living. Driving a car, typewriting, cooking are skills, and sweeping, shoveling, writing, sewing, tying a tie, chopping wood, hammering, etc. In fact, things we do all day are skills we have refined as we matured. Some perform these tasks better than others depending on the desire to improve them and the makeup of the individual personality. Also involved is the amount of obsessive compulsiveness which translates into perfectionism, the level of energy which, if considerable, results in persistence. We also need the intelligence to judge which of our talents are in our best interest and which skills we want to develop that will prove to be rewarding financially, emotionally and spiritually. So the path we take is a matter of choice.

We all do things differently, although the differences may he minor, depending on our idiosyncrasies. Part may be an unconscious control or an instinctive or an inherited capability. In essence, we think it is the sum of individual personality characteristics that produces differences in the way we do things. Thus is provided a means by which we can learn from one another for the benefit of all.

THUMBNAIL SKETCHES OF PERSONALITY TYPES

As each one of us is a unique replica of a human being different from all others, the following sketches of various facets of personality are easily recognizable as we meet people and associate with them through life. There are myriads of combinations. Here are a few.

Some people seem to *enjoy illness,* and find satisfaction in attracting attention by having a chronic physical complaint. They go through life getting a little better, then a little worse, often changing their symptoms. Poor health represents security to them and a release from obligations they dislike, and they find it convenient to use their imaginary illnesses to manipulate others.

Homebodies are extremely passive people and highly inhibited. They feel anxious and insecure when going out alone, so sympathetic relatives encourage them to remain at home where they are comfortable. They are only too glad to take this advice, often for life.

There are some people who approach everything with a *negative* attitude. Nothing is right, everything is wrong or bad. They find pleasure in catastrophic events, like accidents, murders and fires, and derive their pleasure from bad news, which they love to spread about.

Positive thinkers are the opposites of the gloom and doomers, the Pollyanna types who look at the bright side. They sometimes take an unrealistic approach to problems in the belief that everything is going to be or is all right. These are extreme examples and most of us fall in between.

The *chatterbox* never stops talking, usually about himself. He rarely asks a question, but when he does he is off on another tangent before you can reply. Amazingly, he is oblivious of this and most of his talk is a tirade of complaints, criticisms, disapprovals and derogatory inferences. This personality is high in energy, relatively low in intelligence, and with considerable paranoia.

The *quiet type* has a thinking personality and a minimal doing side. Shy by nature, he increases his inhibitions by being hypersensitive. He will never be entirely comfortable in social settings, in spite of his intelligence, which often is high.

Most people have one or two talents and skills they have developed in which they excel, but *generalists* have many. Although they are envied by others, a generalist may find it hard to choose a vocation. For example, a young woman who has abilities for painting also has excellent managerial talent, writes well, and has an innate flair for counseling. She is having difficulty in choosing a career. A middle aged man is proficient in aviation, science and journalism, to name a few of his talents. Having chosen to develop all in turn, he has precluded long term employment in any one field.

Some people are well *organized* and plan everything to the last detail. Their schedules are a model of time management to which they adhere religiously. Their surroundings are equally impeccable. This trait is commendable when it serves the individual, but it ceases to be when it runs him.

Unorganized types are not interested in structure, but they have the same potential for achievement. With high energy, they can accomplish just as much in a helter-skelter way. However, they are not always reliable and have no head for detail.

TO SLEEP, MAYHAP TO DREAM

Freud called dreams "the royal road to the unconscious." Today, medical science questions whether there is an unconscious, and is finding through studies that dreams are undergoing a radical new interpretation. What are these findings? That the brain loses its energy during waking hours, then recharges itself in a reverse operation during sleep.

Who writes the scenarios of our dreams? They are a playback of events that have taken place and serve to ease tension and concern. They are undirected and unrestrained and totally out of the control of the dreamer's mind. They relate to our lives, what has happened and what we fear might happen, but they do not foretell what is going to happen. Dreams are not a revelation of unconscious thought, as some believe. They picture our real feelings and our consciousness, of which we are aware, but sometimes don't like to admit.

We never dream during deep sleep, but only during the "rapid eye movement" period (REM), after we have gone through at least one deep sleep and are about to awaken refreshed. Deep sleeps last from one and a half to two hours, then REM takes over and allows the brain to rewind in order to record another time span of conscious activity. Scientific research shows that all dreams relate to the amount of alpha brain activity that occurs during REM sleep. In studies, subjects were able to move fingers and toes and count the times their bodies were stroked or poked.

Sometimes we have nightmares, which are fright reactions

during sleep. Why are they called that? The dictionary says "a terrifying dream in which the dreamer experiences feelings of helplessness, extreme anxiety, sorrow, etc." Why do we have them? They mirror the fears, anxieties and frustrations we experience in life. Nightmares may occur once or be recurrent. Some are common to many of us, such as being chased by something. We try to run faster but cannot make our legs go, and seem to be losing ground. The terror behind is catching up! The fear and frustration are frightening, until we awaken with pounding heart and fast breathing. What a relief! It's only a dream!

Sometimes we dream of tragedy. Someone we love lies desperately ill, or has died in an accident. We struggle through this and wake up sobbing. The picture is so vivid it haunts us all day. Nothing dispels it or eases the pain, but tomorrow it will be gone. A tragic life event or a traumatic experience, such as in war, can produce recurrent nightmares, causing the dreamer to relive the horror he wants to forget. Hypnosis can dispel these memories by substituting pleasant dreams during a hypnotic trance. Soon the nightmares cease.

Then there is the "striving to achieve" dream. You are climbing a steep mountain or a perpendicular cliff and must reach the top. It's a struggle, and every step seems to make no progress. You hold on to branches and rocks as you go higher and stones come loose and roll past you. You don't dare look down because you are afraid of heights and there is a five hundred foot drop, so you keep looking upward. Ah! you are almost there, and finally reach and climb over the top with a sigh of relief. But alas! You are now faced with the descent on the other side which is also very steep. At this point, you wake up, heart pounding and exhausted, but grateful that it was only a dream.

We all have the sexual dream, and studies indicate that there is a relation between the measure of anxiety and the measure of sexual content. For example, you are with your lover and want desperately to be alone, but are surrounded by people. You whisper together and plot how to find a secluded spot. Everywhere you go, someone pops up or there is no shelter, only open field or no lock on the door and people keep coming in and out. Then it starts to rain and you wake up frustrated and full of desire.

What is a lucid dream? It is the ability to know during a dream that you are dreaming and to direct the scenario into whatever you wish. You can even guide a nightmare into a happy ending and the terror will disperse. You can teach yourself to dream lucidly. This is how. As you awaken, focus on your dream and lie quietly, concentrating on it. Then visualize being asleep within the dream and drift back to sleep. About ten percent of people dream lucid dreams naturally, but anyone can learn how.

Some dreams are pleasant. Have you ever floated through the air in a dream? The experience is fascinating. You are in a crowded room with hundreds of people and you want to move on. You take a deep breath and sail upwards about ten feet over the heads of the crowd, while they look at you in wonder. Then you land gently where you want to. Or you reach a stairway and are in a hurry, so you jump and float slowly down the stairs, landing quietly at the bottom. It's great!

Do men and women dream differently? Yes, in some ways. A recent experiment reveals that women dream more in color and have more emotional dreams than men, and are more often the victims of aggressive dreams. Men dream more about food and less about activity, and more characters are included in their dreams. It was also shown that stressful intellectual activity before sleep can produce anxiety in dreams, and less adaptation on awakening, as compared to more relaxed dreaming not preceded by stress.

IS THERE AN UNCONSCIOUS?

This brings us to the unconscious which, since Freud's time almost a century ago, has been debated ad infinitum, but not as yet scientifically proven. Is there an unconscious? The first scientific studies began in the nineteenth century with Wundt, Titchener, and others, who founded the earliest psychological laboratories. They assumed that the mind could observe its own inner workings. This was studied by trained observers through introspection. However, it was soon found that mental life is not limited to conscious experience, and Heimholtz concluded that conscious perception came from unconscious inferences based on knowledge of the world and memory of past experiences. However, this proved to be merely memory.

Near the turn of the century, Freud and his followers, as well as his opponents, developed the concept that there is an unconscious made up of very distinct parts which more or less control and shape a personality as it develops, and that conscious mental life is determined by ideas, emotions and defenses, all unconscious. Once these precepts were accepted, it was concluded that the unconscious controls and influences thought, action and experience. Thus, the cognitive unconscious became an accepted doctrine.

Scientific work on the conscious and the unconscious was interrupted by the emergence of another group of scientists headed by Watson, who embraced the radical concept of behaviorism, and asserted that consciousness did not exist and behavior was the significant area to focus on. However, this was soon abandoned. Then the "cognitive revolution" took its place in the 1950s, developing into cognitive psychology. Today, this discipline is immersed in the ideology that development, training and experience, in essence, all of life, is controlled by unconscious mechanisms, and that the environment colors these in such a way that we become products of our environment.

Older concepts of mental function did not take the organic nature of the brain into consideration, nor was instinct and heredity important in their determination. We still don't have inconclusive answers, but it is evident that many psychologists have little understanding of heredity, of innate function, or genetic competence. They believe that what you are is how you are nurtured and not how you were born. It's the age old argument of nature versus nurture, and they believe only in nurture, whereas we believe that both have a decisive effect, and nature is the stronger of the two, the force that enables us to function as we do.

Mankind has always been aware that there is something going on inside our heads that we don't understand. We have feelings and thoughts, ideas and pressures. Where do they come from? Why do they suddenly pop into our heads? Why do we feel a certain way one day and the opposite the next? It is the job of modern scientists to determine what forces cause these abstractions. Are they genetic or are they environmentally induced? And what are the sources of the pressures?

These are the questions we must answer. And this should be possible by focusing research along these lines instead of only on the unconscious, which is virtually an amorphous phantom, merely a word. We have just discussed instincts and habits. Does the animal have an unconscious? Or is it just instinct? Are the two equal, separate, totally different or similar and interrelated? Has anything been discovered since

Freud and Jung? Has anything new about the unconscious been turned up. We don't know of any.

We are working on a theory that there is no unconscious. We have instincts, we have a lot of memory, we have habits that we have formed, we have ways of doing things that we don't really think about. And we have a conscience and moral precepts and inhibitions and permissions. In other words, things that we allow ourselves to do and things we don't allow ourselves to do. So we have decision making and choice making all the time. How do we do that? Is it because of unconscious pressures, because of habits, because of our moral precepts and past experiences? We really don't know.

Many of the things we do come from the formation of a habit through learned and repeated behavior. Then the memory picks it up and stores it away. We might also call it an alertness factor, which makes us alert as to what is going on and respond to it without thinking about it, such as being alert to danger, the stove is hot and don't touch it. This is the ever present conflict of thinking and doing about which we have spoken many times. How do you decide to do something? Does the doing influence the thinking or the thinking influence the doing? Is there less thinking to doing than there is to creative thinking or imaginative thinking or fantasy? Or is there as much thinking involved in the doing act or does doing cause thinking? In other words, which came first, the chicken or the egg? All of this is an unknown area and food for thought. For it is the essence of human behavior.

Let us debate learning behavior, such as how did we learn how to walk up the stairs? The stairs are man made. When we were born we didn't know how, so we had to learn and we did. Nobody taught us, we learned by experience, putting one foot after the other as we did when we learned how to walk. A baby learning to walk soon finds out that he has to put one foot after the other or he will fall. And that is how he learned how to go up the stairs. This is behavioral learning experience. Does that come from the unconscious? We, the authors, see it as a learned function and not at all unconscious, and many of these functions have evolved over a period of time from bitter experience so we don't repeat them once we have been burned. Then they become part of our way of life. Such things are not unconscious, they are very conscious, and we add one episode after another to our roster of what works, remember what works and fit it into our needs and practice what works to our advantage and eliminate what doesn't.

This learning experience is similar to what happened to early man, his brain got bigger because it was to his advantage. He learned things that were to his advantage and the more astute he was and the more he calculated and planned ahead and interrelated with the good things, he shook off the bad and kept the good. He found he was better off thus, and his brain grew bigger and he got stronger and more dominant and survived, while those who did not, did not survive.

However, there are pressures within us that cause us to do things at times we don't understand and feel in ways we didn't expect. At times, we may laugh or cry without really knowing why. Is this unconscious reaction? Is this an instinctive response? Is this environmentally induced, is it genetic? Or have we just learned it and forgotten it and a pattern is left in the brain, like a habit? What is really going on? This is a broader, more encompassing question than just the unconscious.

We have regulators of vital functions in our bodies, called autonomic, such as respiration, blood pressure, heart beat, perspiration, sexual feelings, the growth of hair, heating and cooling mechanisms. These take place automatically, and are unconscious on our part. Do these belong to the unconscious? How do we separate them from our basic instincts and genetic tendencies? And how do we separate our unconscious drives from these autonomic functions?

So we start anew. Is there an unconscious, subconscious or nonconscious, as some call it? The consensus is that the unconscious is not what it was thought to be. So what is it? The question is in ferment, and until there is more and deeper research, it will remain in ferment, for at this point our understanding of ourselves, the mind and its functions is not clearly understood, and this touches as well on our philosophy of life and our religiosity. Compare this to extra-sensory perception. This abstract phenomenon has been researched thousands of times by renowned scientists, yet not one example has been proven. So it is with the unconscious.

There is much that we *do* know, however, so let's encapsulate this knowledge. We have thoughts that are not conscious to us. They are instincts, potentials, talents, fears, sensitivities, repressions, loves and hates. Are they in our unconscious, or just stored away waiting to be used? We have memories. Is there a difference between the unconscious and memories, or are they one and the same? And is there a difference between things that are stored to be used and our potentials, instincts, habits and sensitivities? Are these in our unconscious, in our memory or just in us? So we, the authors, have come to the conclusion that there is not an unconscious. Actually, if we had one, our lives would be controlled by it, and it would contain forces we would not recognize as coming from us, and will us to do things we otherwise would not do. This is not a happy thought. Furthermore, the unconscious could become an excuse for letting felons out of crimes they have committed, and allowing sexual mischief. "Don't blame it on him, his unconscious led him to it!" This excuse could he applied to abuse of children, rape, incest and the battering of wives as well as other misdeeds. If we come to believe that our unconscious allows us to commit these evil acts, could we condone them? A resounding NO.

The existence of an unconscious, however, has not been proven and until it is, we need not accept this possibility, for if we did, our lives would not be under our control and indeed we *are* in control of them. The scientists' work is clear. We would like to have them define the genetic structure and the environmental structure once and for all and determine what role nature and nurture plays in the development of personality.

So, until we know more than we do, the question continues, Is there an unconscious? Until that time comes, we should divest ourselves of the fears that have been instilled in us about the unconscious running our lives. Perhaps you have never heard that. You are lucky, for some modern thinkers hold that it is. In our opinion, neither the genetics or the environment or our unconscious runs our lives. *We* run our lives with the help of a mix of the environment and our genetics. But we don't know just what that mix is, whether it is half and half or a third to two-thirds or what. But the more we know about ourselves and our backgrounds, the more we will understand what that mix is. For example, when one person is faced with a challenge he fights, another runs away, another hides and another becomes ill or gives up. For example, there are people whom we consider have strong characters, others are weak and most fall in between. We notice only the extremes, not the in betweens, although every human characteristic is within each one of us to some degree. Therefore, there are numerous ways a person reacts to a challenge, and how he does depends on his mental mix.

So keep an open mind about the unconscious until research comes up with the answers, and put aside the opinions of others and preconceived notions of your own and relax the thought that your environment shaped your personality. Open your mind to the vast inputs of genetic traits that are your heritage, both good and bad, and amuse yourself by piecing together the jigsaw puzzle of the person which is the unique YOU.

4

IN WHAT WAY ARE MEN AND WOMEN DIFFERENT?

The greatest difference between men and women is in the reaction to emotional feelings. Studies show that the physiological effect is similar, but the expression is different and, though the intensity of feeling is equal in men and women, contrary to common impression, men are more deeply affected by emotion than women.

How do women react? They are vocal and express emotion overtly. They weep when sad or hurt, and laugh and giggle when happy. They splatter their feelings about, which relaxes them and enables them to handle the stress. Women are more comfortable with emotion than men and ventilate freely and easily. And when it comes to distress and sadness, women are demonstrative, whereas men hold their feelings inside and are afraid of them. They are extremely sensitive and inhibited by emotion, and consider it unmanly to show how they feel. Ventilating is difficult for them and they seldom resort to it. It is hard for men to deal comfortably with their inmost sentiments; they feel awkward and out of character, so they try to find a way to avoid them if possible. It is less painful that way. It is the same with children. When a mother scolds them, the boys feel guiltier and more repressed than the girls, who argue with their mothers and confront her comfortably. The boys slink off and hide.

Men don't like arguments and shy away from emotional confrontations, rationalizing that they cannot deal with such things in a practical way. When a man comes home from work and senses that his wife has something on her mind, he would rather feed the dog, take the garbage out and fix the lock on the back door than sit down and listen.

When the wife says we have to talk this over, he runs to his workshop in the basement, announcing that he has to finish a job. Why does he act this way! Because he realizes that this is an emotional issue which affects him more strongly than his wife. So he ducks out. He is also afraid he might become emotional, and that is sissified or will evoke hidden passions that he dislikes exposing.

On the other hand, his wife is eagerly awaiting the chance to talk about the issue she is comfortable dealing with and wants to get it settled. Unfortunately, although it is a relief for her to get it over with, she does not realize how painful it is for her husband whom she dearly loves, and that a discussion makes him uncomfortable and builds up stress and tension. As for him, he knows he is out of his element, playing the wrong game on the wrong field and is going to lose. How often does a man win an argument with a woman over an emotional issue? Practically never.

Why do women cope with emotions better than men? This is our theory. Women project toward long-term consequences more than men. They think and plan into the future, and know where they are going because they are less blinded by emotion. They are more practical, and emotion does not block them from focusing on their goals, and they are dedicated toward leading the family toward these goals. A man seems to know instinctively that his wife will direct the family on the appropriate course and trusts her to make wise decisions. His mother always did, so his wife will also. And concurrently, she harasses him to follow her lead, which he usually does.

So, as far as emotions are concerned, women are the professionals and men the amateurs; the women take them in stride and the men are less able to deal with them, so avoid them. This applies to all ages, young children and adolescents included.

Does the environment play a role in these disparities between men and women? This is a matter of debate. One study shows that mothers talk to their little girls more about feelings than to their little boys, which may imply approval to vent them freely. Traditionally, man is not supposed to show emotion, an inhibition society has imposed upon him over the generations.

WE HAVE COMMON TRAITS

Men and women are alike in some ways. One is that all person-alities include both maleness and femaleness. This is primarily to perpetuate the species. Interestingly enough, we all start out female in the early stages of development in the womb. Soon the sex glands are influenced by genes that decide the sex by distributing the genetic coding — XY chromosomes for a boy and XX for a girl. Once this is done, the ovaries and the testes develop, secrete hormones — estrogens and progestins in the female, androgens in the male — and form external and internal genitals. Then, as the baby grows, differences in structure, body build and appearance become visible. Therefore, normally a baby develops as a female unless there are sufficient androgens to influence it. Research confirms this by showing that castration of infant male rats feminizes them, and the administration of androgens to infant female rats masculinizes them. Differences in the brains of the sexes show up in the organiza-tion of neurons and in the parts that affect motivation, emotion, and sexual behavior.

Behavior is different also when monkeys play together, the male is more often dominant, but when females are injected with andro-gens while in the uterus, there is no obvious difference in their behavior from that of the males. Female rats show more activity than males in open spaces, but if male rats are castrated at birth, their activity is indisguishable from that of females. Furthermore, if females are treated with androgens, or have their ovaries removed at birth, their activity is the same as the males. Therefore, these studies show that sex hormones play a part in behavior, and that some behavior can be reversed by the substitution of one hormone with another.

Obviously, we cannot perform these experiments on humans, but studies of female babies who have been inadvertently exposed to androgens before birth show above average interest in athletics and sports and a lack of interest in playing with dolls and engaging in feminine pastimes. They also show a greater than average interest in a career as opposed to marriage and motherhood. Male infants exposed to a high level of female hormones show less than average interest in athletics and sports, low aggressiveness, and delayed sexual development.

So it is inevitable that our sex hormones can be at odds, as the glandular system has a mixture of male and female hormones. So the war between the sexes is virtually being waged within our bodies, as these opposing factions compete with one another. A different concern is the strong nurturing instinct of women, which is also in men but to a lesser degree. Women look for security in order to create the best environment for children, while men are fired by a powerful urge for new experiences and material gain. Thus the struggle reaches into another realm.

Men and women are drawn toward one another primarily to satisfy their needs, but as these are very different, there is bound to be controversy. Opposites, however, continue to attract, regardless of the disparities between them, So disagreements are normal in marriage and serve as a release from tension.

NATURAL SELECTION

The individual choice of a mate is called "natural selection," making possible the improvement of the species. Natural selection is seen in all wild animal life and in most human beings. Many cultures, however, have social and religious rules and traditions whereby parents choose mates for their children. History demonstrates that such cultures become less effective over the centuries and slowly degenerate to the point of extinction, like those of ancient Egypt, Greece and Rome. The fall of a civilization is followed by the rise of a new race that is stronger, unless it too falls victim to the mores that smother natural selection.

Natural selection in humans involves two elements not present in animals. First, the chosen mate is usually someone with a personality similar to that of the parent of one's own sex. In other words, a man is likely to choose a woman whose personality resembles his father's, a woman her mother's. This is, of course, inadvertent. The second element is love, which plays a major role, and enhances the sexual magnetism and physical attractiveness of the love object. While it is not unusual for two good-looking people to pair off, mating is influenced most by a powerful, emotional love, which seems to outweigh beauty, intelligence and social pressures.

It is obvious that over a four million year history, human beings have been evolving toward higher intelligence, greater abilities and longer lives. Thus, natural selection works to advantage.

TIME BRINGS CHANGES

Men and women have conflicting drives. As a rule, women look for the love and support of a man in marriage and the role of bearing and nurturing children. This brings security and a relationship in which, historically, the man is the provider and the woman the primary source of affection and care of the children and the home. While cultural patterns have changed in recent decades, the family remains the basic unit of society, and many women find the traditional role rewarding and sufficient to most of their needs. Others choose a combination of family and career goals, and a minority rule out marriage for other objectives, a few for children without marriage. Each choice produces conflicts for men as well as for women, because it will supplement, coordinate or be in opposition to the male role, and therefore pose problems for one or both partners. The male position has not changed as far as his own pursuits are concerned but it has changed in respect to those of the woman. Over all, men are flexible in accommodating to women who may run the house and a business or hold a job, and even to employment in a competing business or the same office, in which event conflict is apt to arise out of the nature of the work.

So, as a rule, men don't object to their wives working and may even welcome it because of the deterioration of income due to inflation and the desire to maintain modern lifestyle. Consequently, more and more families depend on two incomes, so there no longer is a single financial position, and this results in more divorces in which the woman is being asked to give alimony to the man. Therefore, the need for two incomes, as well as increased potential for the employment of women, has resulted in change in the relationship between husband and wife, so the role change is actually a male/female change.

Today, many men share in the housework and child care, especially when their wives work, but it is important to understand that the nurturing instinct in man is different from that in women. This is a primitive instinct and exists in every form of life, and in human beings, man can have a warm and protective feeling toward the children, but he is not attracted to tiny babies. He will care for the baby and do the usual things to fulfill its needs, but he is doing this primarily to satisfy his wife's needs and thereby receive his quota of love, sex and nurturing.

So the modern role of women results in situations both parties have to adjust to, and men will continue to live their lives as always, which is to accede to the wives' requests and requirements. The consequence is that the woman gets her way nine times out of ten, and the men compensate by bonding together in their clubs and sports and businesses. Women have invaded these areas, however, and men can no longer be free from female contact. For nowadays, women appear to be a part of every activity, even those that formerly were exclusively male.

HOW DO THEY REACT TO SEX?

What are the goals in sexual intercourse? The male goal is for orgasm, the woman's also, but if she does not achieve it, it is not a big deal. Her basic goal is to have a baby, to control her man through his need for her, to establish security and build for the future. The man has none of these objectives. His is to have intercourse with no fringes, and to look forward to the next orgasm. How does a man feel after orgasm? He is somewhat guilty for having gotten away with a pleasurable moment. And the woman? She does not feel guilty, but that she has one up on her partner, whether she succeeds in having an orgasm or not. It gives her a sense of control. A man rarely considers sex as control over a woman.

So the emotional quality of thinking in regard to intercourse is diverse between the sexes. The man plans for his next orgasm, the woman looks into the future for security and at times, a baby.

Although a man's drive to reproduce is less powerful than his sex need, it usually leads to marriage and children. However, part time home life fills this need, and he leaves most of the children's care to his wife. It is a rare man who shares equally in the duties of housekeeping and child care, although this has become more common with the widespread entry of women into the work force. While he is securely attached to his home, man's interests are centered in his job or profession, and in sports and other activities, which are a deep-seated need. This is especially true if he is a doing person, if more of a thinker, he prefers intellectual involvements. In either case, the satisfaction of these interests is his chief motivation, so he feels a tug-of-war between them and home.

MORE DIFFERENCES THAN SIMILARITIES

There are many similarities between the sexes, in intelligence, energy and the intensity of personality characteristics. But there are marked dissimilarities in the thinking and doing areas, and research reveals specific brain variations which are plainly discernible. Several show up in aptitudes for certain tasks, some associated with the emotions and others in sensory keenness.

As a rule, male babies are more curious about objects than people, whereas female babies are engrossed in people, sounds and what is going on around them. Men show from childhood a strong inventive tendency and excel in skills involving depth perception, which makes them more capable in mechanical tasks. Men also show greater ability in mathematics, especially higher mathematics, in which women have difficulty. Women in general have a stronger instinct for language, and in a verbal exchange, the man is usually anxious to terminate the discussion, the woman will continue on and on.

Men have a natural drive to explore and invent and examine unfamiliar objects. This is turned on by a strong curiosity instinct, the basis for problem solving. Women have better finger dexterity and can perform delicate tasks that require hand coordination. They also process information more rapidly, and are more responsive in social settings, which is in keeping with their interest in people.

Emotion is closely bound to the thinking and doing in both sexes—more closely with the thinking in women and the doing in men—and differences in how the brain works show up in the emotional makeup of each. Which sex is the most emotional? Most would say women—but that is wrong. They seem to be, because they show their feelings and verbalize easily, but men are more emotional and pressured by their emotions. Who writes most of the poetry about love? Who gets the most excited at a ball game? Men.

Men exhibit anger readily and throw their weight around; women are slower to react. The talents of art and music are linked to the emotions; the majority of the greatest in these fields are men. An analysis of decisions shows that men are the most swayed by sentiment. Women are more practical, and this flavors decision making. They are less carried away by personal considerations, all of which stems from a strong instinct to nurture and protect the family.

Although women show their emotions, they are in control of them and influenced by common sense and intuition. Their show of emotion is spontaneous and may appear hysterical, which is practical, for they project how they feel. Men seldom show emotion, believing it unmanly, and though their emotions may be stronger and more impulsive, they bottle them up. This can be detrimental to a man who cannot cope with psychological problems, and prevents him from seeking help. Emotional release is healthy, and to do this men are apt to indulge in intense activity, like a sport, fast driving, or a sexual spree.

The nurturing—also called the maternal—instinct is strong in most women and starts in the thinking and is carried out in the doing. Men have it also, but to a lesser degree. It includes the bearing and care of the young, and while the mother-child relationship changes as the child grows into adulthood, the nurturing tie remains, and the spiritual, physical and emotional closeness gradually gives way to a mature concern that lasts throughout life. This extension of concern is not seen in animals', the female rejects the offspring once they are self-sufficient. While women appear to be soft and malleable, as a rule they are strong, and outlive men. This is consistent with their role in caring for children and the preservation of security for the family.

These modern times have brought a change in the care of children and the home. The need for two incomes has produced this, as well as the emancipation of women and their increasing desire to function in the public sector. When the husband and wife both work, the care of the children and the chores of the home have come to be divided between father and mother and sharing the duties of homemaking is a boon to the working wife. This has brought out in men their nurturing instinct, and it is a joy to watch a daddy with an infant in his arms.

Families of single parents with children have increased enormously. Most are women but some are men, and they have the more difficult task. Hopefully, each has a relative or a close friend who can lighten the burden until the children are in school. Society has come a long way in the past few decades.

The sexes differ in remembering the past and planning for the future. Men forget past trouble and women remember it. Women have negative memories, but positive hopes for the future, whereas men look back on pleasant occasions and dread what may come. This helps prepare women for emergencies and worrisome episodes that occur, such as illnesses of the children.

DIFFERENCES IN THE SENSES

Men have better daylight vision, while women see better at night. Women have better hearing and less tolerance for loud sounds—eighty-five decibels seems twice as loud as it does to men. Men have less sensitive taste buds and a greater liking for highly seasoned and strong tasting foods. There seems to be no difference in the sense of smell, the degree of which is individual. Women are more sensitive to heat and less to cold, probably because they have an extra layer of fat. Touch, however, is another matter. Women are more stimulated by touch than men. They are extremely responsive to a lover's caresses, while men seldom look for this kind of stimulation.

DREAMS

Men and women have essentially the same kinds of dreams; the dream of running from a pursuer, the falling dream, the flying dream, the embarrassing dream, the sexual dream. These are remarkably similar in all people, but women dream in color more than men. Women are more sensitive to what a dream may mean and likely to consider it as an emotional sign or a prophecy. Men don't think about the meaning of dreams.

AGGRESSION AND PASSIVITY

Men and women differ in passivity and aggression only in degree. We associate aggression with men and passivity with women, but women can be just as aggressive and men just as passive. The real difference lies in how it is used. When a man and a woman argue, the more aggressive attacks the passive; the woman, as aggressor, uses words; the man may harass her physically. Physical aggression is usually attributed to a man, but the verbal attack of a woman can be just as painful.

Male aggression is an offensive drive to obtain something a man wants—a woman, possessions or social status. It is closely linked to the sex drive, and also shows up in business, sports and competition. Since primitive times men have fought to protect family and home and for sexual and material possessions. Evolution and civilization have added a new dimension to this urge to dominate but only in man does it lead to the death of opponents.

The link between the sex drive and violent drive is almost exclusively male. Some areas in the brain control sexual aggression, others simple aggression, and others anger and hostility. The nerve centers of these areas interrelate in ways not fully understood, and sometimes an aggressive drive builds up to a point that ends in a crime. While women have been known to kill, it is rare. Most crimes of violence are committed by men.

When is a woman more aggressive than passive? Rarely does she feel compelled to do physical injury, but she will fight savagely for her children, and go to her physical limit to protect them, but she does not want to go to war, nor does she want to kill. Revenge is in the form of verbal attacks.

Some women show their aggressiveness through belittling, being catty, baiting, or spreading vicious gossip. They are also skilled at manipulation—another form of aggressiveness and closely linked to paranoia—working through the male to accomplish what they want. Men are often susceptible and willing targets. When observing married couples, it is evident that the wife usually gets her way and seems to "wear the pants." Greek and Roman history is filled with incidents of "the power behind the throne", the emperor's wife.

Animals are aggressive for the same reasons as men: to protect themselves, the females and their territory. However, there is one difference; combat is seldom to the death, for no animal kills for revenge or to ward off a future threat. Its primary purpose is to select the fittest male rather than eliminate the weaker. This enhances the breeding potential of the species and safeguards against congenital mutations and crippling genes.

Female animals show aggression while nurturing their young, no creature is fiercer than at this time. They do not want protection by males, who are largely excluded. Some male birds feed their young, and some fish help protect them, but these are the exceptions. They are generally considered a threat by the females, for most male animals do not identify with their offspring at any stage, but see them as invaders and potential threats, and only the female can recognize her young by scent.

Passivity too can be effective and is just as common as aggression, and both sexes use passive techniques to reach a goal. Women use it oftener than men, because they are weaker physically. They also are skilled in the indirect approach, like giving in unexpectedly or putting on an image of pity—"clinging vine" technique. They have little guilt about winning by wiles and devious means, which has baffled men through the ages!

For example, a woman took charge of a manufacturing company, assuming the position that had been vacated by a man, and confronted the all-male employees with: "If you don't want to work for a woman, speak up now and I will accept your resignation." All remained loyal.

Another example, a woman executive hired a man as managing director. She could see that their swords might soon cross, so she played the helpless role: "I don't have your engineering expertise nor your way with the employees, so I will depend on you a good deal." This made him feel that he was in charge.

The use of passivity is defensive, self-serving and self-promoting. It is often the best strategy and a man may use it when he realizes that it will take him farther, and it is often the technique of choice, especially in business and social situations. When you decline an unwanted invitation by saying your wife is ill, you are using passivity. Supposedly, you are protecting her, but actually you are hiding behind her.

An overly passive man may choose a field in which there is little competition. He is polite to his boss, even though he is angry, and tries to please by doing little things for him. He is careful to avoid confrontations and adroit at substituting passive means to gain his end. A good analogy is when an animal, having lost the fight, lies down and plays dead.

The environment plays a significant role in the development of principles and standards. In our society, boys are trained to be little men and girls to be little women, however, maleness and femaleness directs sexual evolvement and this will emerge eventually. While parental, social and peer example can also play a part in molding a child's character, nothing can change his basic personality.

VIVE LA DIFFERENCE!

The most marked differences between men and women are the aggressive quality in men and their primary focus on objects, and the nurturing quality in women with emphasis on people. But there is no hard and fast rule. Many men, like chefs, tailors, typists, nurses, and dress designers, have skills usually attributed to women, while women become executives, architects, dentists and mathematicians. There are men who are deeply concerned about people and women who are not. So men and women can go as far as their capabilities allow, with no restrictions on gender. The true criterion is ability.

5

HOW TO KNOW YOUR OWN AND INTERPRET OTHER PERSONALITIES

Now you have an understanding of what a personality is comprised of and can put together the elements of yours. The questionnaires in this chapter will help you decide.

First, start with the four cornerstones, thinking, doing, energy and intelligence. Are you more of a thinker than a doer or vice versa? These add up to one hundred percent and it is the rare person who has fifty percent of each. Most of us are somewhat one sided and tend to favor the dominant side to the neglect of the other. It's easy to slip into such a lifestyle, but there is a balance, and finding the right balance takes effort, but it is worth it.

Review the first few pages of this book and unless you already have made a decision, you will find a clue as to which is your dominant side. The basics are that the more thinking person, although he is into both, is more into things than people, and prefers to engage in activities of a more intellectual bent such as reading, writing and going to museums and art shows. He does, however, like to socialize, engage in sports and have fun, but not as much as the more doing person. He is apt to be a workaholic and should watch this trend and not drive himself and enjoy life a bit. The more doing person is outgoing and likes to be with people and have fun. He may let socializing or a game of tennis interfere with responsibilities. He finds routine duties a burden although he carries through with them under secret duress. The thinker rather enjoys his routine tasks.

This test should help in establishing your degree of thinking and doing. Most probably you have more of one than the other, but this is difficult to decide, because we switch quickly back and forth and it's impossible to measure the amount of time we "think" and the amount of time we "do". However, you can arrive at a fairly accurate estimation which should be sufficient, and answering these questions will help.

THINKING	YES	NO	NOT REALLY
Are you sensitive to the needs of others?	___	___	___
Do you emphasize the intellectual over the physical?	___	___	___
Are you more interested in things than in people?	___	___	___
Do you prefer to solve problems yourself or would you rather let others solve them?	___	___	___
Are you more interested in the long term benefits at the sacrifice of the immediate return?	___	___	___
Do you mask your emotions with rationalizations?	___	___	___
Do you like order and neatness in your surroundings?	___	___	___
Do you feel comfortable with routine?	___	___	___
Are you conscientious in daily tasks?	___	___	___
Do you prefer your own company to the company of others most of the time?	___	___	___
Do you consider yourself a loner?	___	___	___

DOING	YES	NO	NOT REALLY
Would you rather be doing something in order to avoid the intellectual?	___	___	___
Do you take short cuts to goals?	___	___	___
Do you sometimes act impulsively?	___	___	___
Are you comfortable in a disorderly setting?	___	___	___
Do you enjoy parties and socializing more than being alone?	___	___	___

Are you apt to put your needs before
those of others? ____ ____ ____
Do you spend your leisure time
having fun and recreation? ____ ____ ____
Are you bored by routine duties? ____ ____ ____
Do you like people better than things? ____ ____ ____
Would you rather play golf or
tennis than visit a museum? ____ ____ ____
Do you balk at daily tasks and
sometimes neglect them? ____ ____ ____

The total of "yeses" and "nos" indicates the relation of thinking to doing. An equal degree of each shows extreme versatility and an endowment with talents in several fields.

There is more to our thinking, which has many facets, and probably the most important one is how we think with the right and left sides of the brain, as described in Chapter 2. The left brain is flexible and open, the right brain rigid. The ability to switch from right to left and back can have a significant influence on daily living, but most people can't do this readily, nor do they know how. However, it can be learned with practice and comes in very handy in decision making and problem solving and in situations that crop up unbeknownst. So practice switching. It's a useful skill and makes life easier.

We can find out with which side of the brain we are thinking by answering these questions.

LEFT BRAIN THINKING   <u>YES</u>   <u>NO</u>   <u>NOT REALLY</u>

Do you have an open mind? ____ ____ ____
Can you change your views and
habits easily? ____ ____ ____
Do you listen to discussions that don't
reflect your point of view? ____ ____ ____
Do you like change per se? ____ ____ ____
Can you accept ideas and opinions
that don't coincide with yours? ____ ____ ____
Do you accept innovations in
business and social life and
give them a chance to work? ____ ____ ____

RIGHT BRAIN THINKING

	YES	NO	NOT REALLY
Are you set in your ways and not interested in changing them?	___	___	___
Is it hard for you to accept the ideas of others?	___	___	___
Does it bother you to have to change your schedule?	___	___	___
Do you argue with opposing points of view?	___	___	___
Are you tenacious about certain habits and find it hard if you have to change them?	___	___	___
Are your political opinions set in concrete?	___	___	___
Do you believe deeply in your religion and disparage other religions?	___	___	___

These are characteristics some of us may want to change and now may be the time to do so. Practice the thinking from right to left brain and back again and you will find it rewarding.

A PERSONALITY CANNOT BE CHANGED

Speaking of change, it must be remembered that we are referring to change in thinking, not in personality, for this we cannot change, either in ourselves or in another person. Some people try to shape another into a mold of their choice, but this is impossible. But have we not changed over the years? Have we not improved in many ways and developed understanding? Has not self management increased, intelligence blossomed and are we not more adept at meeting life's demands? The answer is, of course, yes, but these are modifications in personality, not changes. Over the years we perfect our self-images by understanding ourselves better, both our virtues and our faults. Then, we can work on the traits we don't like until we feel comfortable with what we are.

Here is an example of how self understanding can work. One of the authors has a patient who had difficulty relating to other people. She is an intelligent woman with high principles but is critical of most people, believing she is helping them. After sharing the above facts with her, a month later she returned. She had concluded that she has high energy, more paranoia than is good, and believes this was causing her problems. She is aware that she is very critical, yet cannot take criticism or accept suggestions, and always tries to impose her opinions on her friends, feeling that they are best. Furthermore, she is afraid people are talking about her and therefore she trusts no one. Having come to this decision, she began to modify her paranoia and today, she is a happier person.

If we cannot change our personalities, what should we do to be a better person? It would be nice if we were able to change, but this is not possible so we have to settle for shaping and revamping them in order to adapt to all the aspects of life with which we have to contend each day. We constantly direct ourselves toward the various sectors, first one and then another. There is work, finances, home and social life, recreation and sexual behavior. There are multiple angles and decisions that must be made for each, whether we are playing a game of tennis or engaged in selling a nuclear power plant. We do this every day and each demands a special mix of attributes that must be conjured up and utilized in order to be successful. Conforming such as this, however, does not change our personalities. They were born in us and stay the same through life, but we can learn to understand the way they interact in relationships and in the management of our lives.

Basic characteristics never change either, but we can learn to know what they are and utilize our strong points, avoid the weak ones, and build up those that need strengthening. We can soften the paranoid and hostile elements and increase the effectiveness of good ones. So it is a matter of management rather than of change, and important to accept that we cannot change personality, ours or anyone else's. No one else can either, nor therapy nor psychiatric or psychological counseling of any kind. However, therapy can help us understand better. The color of hair and eyes, the stature and body build and the shape of hands and feet stay with us for life, and this is true of personality as well. The only way it can be changed is by injury to the brain.

We may wonder how we can build up our weak points and increase the effectiveness of our good ones. This is possible, but it takes self-insight, which most people don't have, however, it can be supplied by the input of a good friend. It is a question of self evaluation, actually self analysis, and to accomplish this it's almost essential to have the objective assessment of another person. So we have devised a simple test which a friend can review and advise on regarding the strong and the weak points.

Are you doing well with people and poorly with material things?

Are your actions successful but your thoughts lacking?

Is your sexual life inhibited but your creative life good?

Are you accomplishing what you want to in life?

Are you spending too much time in fruitless pursuits?

Are your interests mostly intellectual but your friends are disappearing?_____
Are you doing more than you should in the thinking area?

Making the effort to bolster a weakness offers a feeling of satisfaction similar to the mild euphoria experienced by a thinker who goes jogging or a doer who relaxes with an interesting book.

INTELLIGENCE
There is no way we can test intelligence on these pages. It takes a trained psychologist to administer a battery of tests, but it is possible to come to a rough estimation through past scholastic records and life achievement to date. The actual level of intelligence can be ascertained by tests for the intelligence quotient. Refer to Chapter 1 for more information.

ENERGY
Finding energy level is an easier task. Again, Chapter 1 describes this characteristic in detail, but answering these questions will give a clue to the answer.

	YES	NO	NOT REALLY
Do you wake up in the morning ready to tackle the day with vigor?	___	___	___
When on an errand, do you walk fast?	___	___	___
When you walk with a friend, do you set a fast pace?	___	___	___
Are you a fast talker?	___	___	___

Do you prefer the fast lane in life?   ___   ___   ___
When you are going somewhere, are you the
  one who is impatient to leave?   ___   ___   ___
Do you write fast and are you anxious to
  finish a sentence?   ___   ___   ___
Do you have fast reactions when you drive
  a car?   ___   ___   ___
When moving about the office or house, are
  you quick in your actions?   ___   ___   ___

These questions relate to high energy, and are readily observable in yourself or another person. If yours is a slower pace, your level of energy can be determined from the questions on a descending scale. And energy can vary throughout the twenty-four hours, depending on how the biological clock is set which has nothing to do with the basic level of energy. Some people are slow starters in the day and others awake and running early. This occurs fairly often in married couples, one of whom is an early riser and tired at night, and the other slow to arise and lively at night. The husband falls asleep at nine o'clock and the wife wants to go out partying. In the morning, he is lively and gets going early and she cannot budge. They both may have the same level of energy, but they are geared to using it at different hours of the day. The biological clock is explained later in this chapter.

PASSIVENESS AND AGGRESSIVENESS
Now, let's discuss the additional characteristics we have which remain in the background waiting to be needed. Whether we call on passiveness or aggressiveness and the amount we use is largely determined by the level of our other traits, such as paranoia, energy, doing and thinking, so they cannot be judged until the circumstance arises that requires them. Suffice it to say that self observation can tell how well or poorly these qualities are applied depending on the outcome of the situation.

Again, if memory fails, refer back to Chapter 1. We may have a preponderance of one or the other and usually aggression is attributed more to men than women, but women can be just as aggressive, only in a different way, verbally, not physically, which usually is ascribed to men. Taking things lying down is a sign of being unduly passive and if we are too passive we can be taken advantage of, but inordinate aggression is unacceptable and alienates us from friends and colleagues.

These traits can be controlled so they don't get out of hand, and it is more difficult to curb aggression than passivity, however, passivity can also serve to gain a point. We must judge each situation as it arises before deciding which to use and how much.

OBSESSIVE COMPULSIVENESS

This is our fussy quality. The obsessive compulsive person is neat and tidy and the disorderly person has little of this element.

The degree possessed can be proven fairly well by these questions. The "yeses" have it, the "nos" do not; the "not really's" are average.

	YES	NO	NOT REALLY
Are you particular about your grooming and want it always perfect?	___	___	___
Are you the most content when wearing comfortable,casual clothes and dislike dressing up?	___	___	___
Are you uncomfortable when your surroundings are untidy and things out of place?	___	___	___
Are you meticulous about washing your hands and keeping your nails manicured?	___	___	___
Do you mind when your hands are dirty?	___	___	___
Are you a sloppy housekeeper?	___	___	___
Do you keep your desk in order?	___	___	___
Do you mind if it is a mess?	___	___	___

PARANOIA IS A TWO-EDGED SWORD

We all have some paranoia as does every living thing. In small amounts, it poses risks, in moderate amounts, it is our protective element, a high degree breeds unpopularity, in excess it can be destructive. Fortunately, this last few people have. The term "paranoid" has come to be used in a derogatory sense, narrowing its meaning. How do we know how much we have? Ask yourself these questions, the first part means high paranoia, the second low.

Are you suspicious of people or are you trusting?

Are you resentful at times almost to hostility, or easy going?

Do you fear the unknown or are you unafraid to the point of foolishness?

Are you afraid of taking chances such as in a business deal or a physical activity in which you could be hurt, or do you put yourself at unnecessary risk?

Do you suspect that people are working against you, or do you trust most people?

Do you want everything signed, sealed and delivered, or do you take people at their word?

Are you inclined to criticize others, or are you open to criticism?

Do you resent being criticized or do you accept it gracefully?

Are you compelled to control people or are you amenable to others taking over?

Do you consider your ways of doing things to be superior, or do you listen to the opinions of others?

Do you blame others for your mistakes or do you take the blame?

Do you thirst for power, or do you let another enjoy it?

Do you feel that people are watching your comings and goings or don't you care if they are?

THE BIOLOGICAL CLOCK

There are many facets of personality other than those described which are not relevant here. They are mood swings, intellectual leanings, financial abilities, spiritual tendencies, musical and artistic talents, athletic skills and the capacity for sexual arousal. But what is relevant are the internal mechanisms we have within our bodies, such as differences in body chemistry and a biological clock. It is a timing device that controls the metabolic function of the body, thereby accomplishing a number of necessary processes.

First, is the electrochemical performance of the brain, then the chemical and endocrinologic functions of the body, and third, the muscular and motor activities followed by the less conscious actions such as sleep, heart rate, digestion and so forth. These functions color personality in ways such as how we feel when we wake up, and how much sleep we need, and the status of well-being at the time. All reflect on how we act. Also involved are functions such as blood sugar, hemoglobin, oxygen levels and other functions, and most important is the amount and quality of nutrients taken in to fuel them. So, if there is high brain energy with a high metabolic rate, a person can operate at full efficiency for long periods of time, provided the body is sufficiently supplied with nutrients. These internal functions are inborn and remain with us for life. Thus, with enough mental and physiologic activity and the correct combination of oxygen, food, minerals and fluid, a person can deliver his maximum output, considering his maximum potential.

This sounds as though our biological clocks are mechanical and run like quartz timepieces. But this is not the case, for emotion and changes in mood affect both mental and bodily functions, in turn affecting body chemistry, which feeds back to increase or reduce the efficiency of whatever we are doing, whether we are talking to someone, reacting to an emotional experience or having a confrontation or a religious discussion. Whatever we are doing can be influenced or influence the deeper functions that interrelate with our actions.

A classic example is the case of a couple who came to one of the authors for advice about their marriage. On questioning, it was ascertained that the husband had high energy in the morning and was exhausted at night. He would jump out of bed at six o'clock, full of vim and vigor, bright eyed and bushy tailed and tear off to work with enthusiasm. In the evening, he would come home, ask when would dinner be ready and settle down to the evening paper in a comfortable chair. Once dinner was over, he went right to bed and to sleep.

The wife's biological clock worked the opposite way. In the morning, she was slow waking up and was lethargic most of the morning, slowly building up energy to a peak in the afternoon. By the time her husband got home, she was anxious to go out and have an evening on the town or visit friends or entertain at home. It was obvious that this couple was very poorly suited. They fought all the time and the diverse output of energy interfered with their sexual enjoyment and their social life, as well as intellectual communications between them. It also affected the opportunity to share many things of mutual value. The discrepancy in the timing of their biological clocks was at the bottom of their problem, because they were set at different rates and timing.

A situation such as this does not preclude a couple from being happily married. What it takes is understanding and acceptance of these differences between them and that there may be certain activities they cannot share because of the crisscross surges of energy, which can occasion material for conflict and prevent closeness that otherwise would have taken place. We have known many couples with this problem who have solved their marital difficulties this way.

Strangely enough, there are people with severe physical disorders such as paralysis, who are able to produce remarkable intellectual feats because their mental energy is so high it allows them to overcome the physical deficits. It seems as though their physical energy has migrated to the brain and augmented the brain's regular quota. And by the same token, others with distinctive physical attributes produce miserable results because of inadequate mental capacity or weak moral principles. They dissipate their energies in worthless, destructive or even criminal conduct.

LIKES AND DISLIKES

Everybody has likes and dislikes. Some are deeply seated and at times we project them openly without being aware. There are those who don't like dark haired people, or blondes or certain racial or religious types. Some favor tall people, and others have an aversion to white or black people. To others, some are too fat or too thin.

So there are tremendous differences in what appeals to us and what we have an aversion to, and all are built into the human psyche. The mixtures of these qualities filter into interpersonal relationships and can cause a pleasant, mutually, profitable liaison or block it completely. The present situation regarding gay rights is an example. Homosexuals are sensitive, easily frustrated, easily aroused and pressed into hysterical behavior, whereas some "straight" people have difficulty coping with the concept of homosexuality and become biased against it.

Most of us don't condone prejudice, but everyone has likes and dislikes and, no matter how hard we try to erase them, they continue to be entrenched in our psyches. If we are careful to keep them submerged, these antagonisms remain unknown, and we keep them to ourselves, whether they have to do with personality traits, the way people look, their skin color, their religious or political beliefs, their language or the way they dress. These elements may be superficial and not the fault of the individual, or present for life and irreversible. Such feelings are powerful forces within us and should be well understood, so we can modify our attitudes and get along better in our world.

The antithesis of this is an immediate awareness that we like someone upon first meeting. We take to them without knowing why. Could it be compatible internal chemistry? We don't know. But we do know that this happens and that it has nothing to do with the characteristics of a particular individual. So we can only conclude that balance is an important factor in personal relationships as well as in how we manage life.

Races evolved in this way by prejudicial selection, such as darker people marrying darker people, and it is speculated that we all started as one color. This is true because the blood, tissues and organs of the human race are interchangeable, regardless of race, color, background, nationality, religion or sexual preference. But we should not be criticized for having preferential feelings, and for being more comfortable with certain kinds of people and uncomfortable with others.

Where does it come from? It appears to be hereditary, stemming from a deep sense of family, and may start with sibling rivalry which translates into competition in business, social relationships, religious and political tenets or whatever. It is built into everyone, and we think it is a deep primitive instinct competing for survival. It goes back to earliest childhood and could be construed as competing for food. As the child matures, the instinct grows, invades human intellect and translates into aspirations for power, money and fame. Then religious and philosophical thinking interferes and reminds us that we have been taught to "love thy neighbor as thyself" and we must not be prejudiced or challenge anyone, while all the time these dictums don't fit in with what we feel or think. Where did they come from? They were born in us when a primitive society and put there for survival. We don't need them any more but they persist in still being there.

And most importantly, we should not deny our primitive instincts, the good and the bad, which at times may bother us. Some will be hostile and some compassionate, some will be friendly and some unfriendly, and we may want to dominate and take possession. We may have sexual feelings that shock us and sneaky feelings we don't like to admit. How can we handle these mixed emotions? Be honest with ourselves, nurture the good ones and curb the bad ones, but admit them all. Self knowledge is essential to self control.

HOW DO WE INTERPRET OTHER PERSONALITIES?

Now that you have a good idea of your own personality, use the same formula in interpreting another's. Usually, determining the four cornerstones plus the degree of paranoia is sufficient. Be sure to understand yourself first.

In your opinion is this person more of a thinker or a doer? Is he more into things or people? As some people say, a things person or a people person. Is his energy high, moderate or low. Does he talk fast, move and walk quickly and use hands and body in a lively manner, or are his movements moderate and speech rather slow. Perhaps he has really low energy, which you can spot by the languid way in which he moves and a measured manner of speaking.

In order to determine thinking and doing, refresh your memory by the questionnaire on your own personality, then question him about his habits and what he likes best to be doing. This will expedite your decisions.

Intelligence is not easy to determine until you have an opportunity to delve into a person's mind. Start by bringing up subjects that may be of mutual interest, such as current issues in politics and the status of the world. Ask him what his hobbies are, if he likes music and what sports he follows. Is he interested in art and the theatre. Ask him what he does for a living and what his ambitions are. Queries of this nature will disclose his level of intelligence.

Now, figure out the degree of paranoia your subject has. During your conversation, did he agree with anything you said? Or did he give the impression that his ideas and opinions are better? Did he seem suspicious, even slightly hostile? Or did he listen quietly without interrupting. Was he trying to control the discussion or did he allow you free rein? You might want to refer to the questionnaire on paranoia in order to refresh your memory on the signs of high paranoia.

In order to know another personality we must learn how to adjust our thinking. This takes flexibility, so keep the left brain tuned in. How can I do this? Put on the thinking cap of someone with whom you disagree and try to think as he does. Then switch back to your own thinking. Thus, you can learn to adopt a style to fit the personality of the person you are dealing with and you will both be comfortable. But if you let your personality take its course without adjusting to the other, it is like a spirited horse, uncontrolled, paying no attention to the reins. This may antagonize people and get you into trouble in a personal relationship.

A basic premise in knowing another person is to observe what he does and not to judge him by what he says. In other words, come to know him by his deeds and, because most of us don't abide by this, we continually fall for someone's line. We find this in business, in romance and in all personal relationships where the individual with a gift of gab barges his way into situations he would never have been allowed in were it not for his persuasive chatter. Some people, the proverbial "con" men, can fool others with words, but only deeds speak the truth. However, listening is also important, because by listening we can get an idea of intelligence, vitality and a hint of sincerity. But sincerity, honesty and the quality of morality can only be judged through actions.

As already stated, the determination of the four cornerstones and the degree of paranoia is sufficient to evaluate the character of most people, but if you wish to go into depth, find out which of these elements it has as well. Is it rigid or permissive, overbearing or sweet, controlling, compassionate, aggressive, hostile, passive, giving or a combination. Is this person strong minded, suspicious, hypercritical, weak or belligerent. If so, accommodate yourself to him and be sturdy enough so you are not prevailed upon to agree to something you don't want. As we said, flexibility in thinking can be cultivated, then we can adjust to another personality and compare it to ours.

You may run up against hostility, and the way to handle it is to suggest a common cause. Find something you both agree upon, promote and encourage it. This gentle manipulation works well when you are confronted by an angry person, and especially if you are dealing with a paranoid, which usually winds up in conflict. Finding a common agreement will make him feel comfortable, at least temporarily, and allow you to complete the business at hand. This method can be applied to all relationships, personal, business, recreational, or whatever. This requires astute observation and communication. It takes knowing yourself and being able to recognize qualities in the other person.

Without realizing it, we are trying to figure people out every day as we go about our business. Why does he do that instead of this; why does she talk that way? And the answers are wrong most of the time because we don't know how, and we are apt to make false assumptions. Most people cannot communicate well enough to negotiate in a satisfactory manner, so a great many blunder along innocently, being used or using others. Perhaps a half get their way through manipulation, a few control everyone and make others pay for their actions. These are the paranoids. It is they who make the rules and set up the organization and dominate. Such people make few friends, and even those drop away as time goes on, however, most are productive and the world needs them.

How does a couple resolve differences in personality? Through communication with open discussion. Thus, the hassles that are bound to occur in marriage can be placated, and knowing one another well is the key to solving them. However, both parties must be willing to play the game.

So how do we identify better with people? Get to know their personalities. This opens the door to understanding, and understanding gives rise to tolerance, which is the link in the chain to mutually satisfying relationships. Remember, know your own personality first, then go about knowing the other person's.

EXAMPLES OF COMBINED TRAITS OF PERSONALITY

There are as many combinations of personality traits as there are people on this planet. Here are a few.

Thinking with low energy. A more thinking person with high intelligence and low energy rarely realizes his productive potential. As a businessman, he may be deeply involved in making money, as a poet or artist, he aspires to do great work. In neither case is he likely to succeed, because of his tendency to go off on a tangent, and he constantly berates himself for his inability to achieve his goals. He is criticized for laziness or failure to contribute, but he is really suffering from the results of low energy.

Doing with low energy. The person with strong doing tendencies, high intelligence and low energy enjoys working with people. He has high ambitions, but is unable to fulfill them due to his trouble in coping on a day to day basis. He is inclined to be addictive, and frustrations about his ineffectuality can turn him to alcohol or drugs. He excuses himself for his mistakes and failures, blaming them on others or on circumstances. His self-image is that of an idealist who is constantly thwarted in his good intentions.

Society would have difficulty functioning without the many *doing people with low intelligence and low energy.* They perform menial and less demanding jobs in business, industry and civil service, as file clerks, couriers, waitresses, domestics, street sweepers, garbage men, and ditch diggers. These people tend to be right brain thinkers, and find it hard to change their habits, which contributes to their reliability. The world needs them.

Thinkers and doers with low energy are people who don't fend for themselves. They seem unable to cope with life and take advantage of the handouts offered. They live on welfare from one generation to the next and seem content to occupy the lowest echelon of society as long as they don't have to take care of themselves. They could work at menial jobs, many of which go begging, but they excuse themselves on the grounds of illness, disability or lack of training.

Thinkers and doers with excessive passivity are the people who desperately need a leader with whom to identify. They become wedded to the church or join some sect or cult where they find an individual who can tell them where to put their energies and their money and counsel them on how to manage their lives. Regardless of their intellectual or energy levels, they cannot cope alone.

Some don't relate to other persons and are virtual loners. Like the born again Christian groups, they prefer an idealized leader about whom they can fantasize.

Thinkers with high energy are successful in many fields. Scientists like William Teller and Albert Einstein had this kind of personality. They also were endowed with high intelligence. Picasso, Beethoven and Bach are examples in the field of art. Margaret Mead had this makeup, and didn't limit her talents to private practice, but extended them into public life.

High energy thinkers share an aptitude for precision and detail. They are generally creative and happy people, absorbed in their books, figures or research, working out ways to improve the world.

Doers with high energy are egocentric and demanding. Their intelligence level determines the extent of their achievement, but high drive and doing qualities can make them unscrupulous and irresponsible. They think more of themselves than of others, are very extroverted, and good at socializing, especially if it is to their advantage. A personality like this makes a top notch salesman.

PERSONALITIES IN COUPLES

When both partners are the *thinking type, one with high energy and one with low,* they clash continually, because the energetic wants to share intellectual interests and the other has not the vigor, therefore not the will. The resultant conflicts are detrimental to the marriage and are aggravated by the similarity of their thinking qualities.

Suppose *one is a thinker, the other a doer and both have high energy.* The husband is an intellectual who wants to spend his time in science, medicine or law. His wife is interested in people, parties and social events. She also likes sports, which he finds boring. She may drink too much at parties, which he resents. She can be irresponsible about household chores, whereas he is exceedingly neat. Although a good mother, she is more inclined to follow her interests, leaving much of the child care to her husband. While their sex life may be compatible, it is difficult for these two to make a lasting marriage.

This couple has comparable *doing and high energy* qualities. They probably don't focus on children, although they may have one or two. They are both life-of-the-party types and fairly heavy drinkers. They have a good time together. If he has to work, he chooses an occupation like sales that involves people and suits his need for excitement. If he has money, he doesn't work. His wife is likely to neglect the house and is seldom at home, caught up in a round of shopping, sports and social events. This couple will probably burn out, tire of one another and divorce.

Both husband and wife are *highly intelligent, both are thinking types with high energy.* One is a chemist, the other a professor of English. They enjoy their work and are successful. However, their lives are one sided except for occasional socializing with colleagues. They know few people outside the university and are not interested in expanding their acquaintance. Their two children are bright and will probably follow in their parents' footsteps.

Husband and wife are much alike, *intelligent, thinkers, but with low energy.* They may be writers or teachers, but lacking sufficient drive to study for advanced degrees, they remain in low paying jobs. While they have many plans for the future and desires for change, they never seem to complete a project. If one partner is less intelligent, he is content to remain in a primary or high school teaching position year after year. Their marriage is compatible and solid.

One is a thinker and the other a doer, both have low energy. This should be a stable marriage with few conflicts. Opposites in thinking and doing attract, and produce children with varied personality makeups, resulting in variety at home and a healthy balance of thinkers and doers. The thinking member of this team may be a teacher, a writer, or some other kind of low key intellectual, while the doer, if the wife, probably does not work. Their main problem is the lack of mutual interests.

This couple are both *doers, one with high, the other with low energy.* Regardless of the similarity in doing, they have conflicts because of the difference in energy levels. They both like people but the wife is reluctant to entertain because it is such an effort. Where she may agree to one set of tennis, her husband holds out for three or four.

This couple are *both doers with low energy.* One has higher intelligence, but the low energy inhibits its use. Both are fond of sports and socializing. Neither will develop talents to any significant degree. They can have a compatible marriage and enjoy life in a leisurely fashion. Their children will probably be another generation of doers, and if one is endowed with higher energy, he could give them trouble during adolescence.

What is the blend of personality characteristics that will ensure a compatible and lasting marriage? This is difficult to determine and we know of no combination that is ideal. The best formula is for husband and wife to have similar personalities, with fairly comparable levels of energy, paranoia and intelligence. Unfortunately, alikes don't often attract, opposites usually do, unless a strong sexual pull brings them together.

6

SEXUALITY

WHAT IS SEXUALITY?

Sexuality is the manifestation and conduct of our sex drive and the associated emotions—how we think, how we feel, and how we act. It is one of the three governing forces—the others, self-preservation and self-advancement. They are vitally important and interact together, influenced by personality.

There is an ever present undercurrent of sexuality in our thinking, even though there are times when the nourishment of the body and its care are uppermost or we may be concentrating on our careers or social and financial security. Then energy flows to fill these needs and we give little attention to anything else. However, our sex drive is always at work, flavoring our actions. We are constantly aware of the opposite sex and are proud of being a man or a woman. We show this in the way we dress and how we act, and when the mind is free to wander, it invariably comes up with sensual thoughts. There are times when it comes forward and totally dominates, and even a healthy sexuality may take precedence to the degree that it runs our lives.

Sexuality is always present in any interchange between a man and a woman. It can range from a casual glance between strangers to sexual intercourse. It crosses over all age lines, and can be observed in infants as the author did with fascination as she held her eight months old daughter while greeting guests. She was intrigued to notice that the baby concentrated her gaze on the men and passed over the women!

In the past, many religions held rigid positions on sexual morality, and maintained that sex was intended for reproduction and to indulge in it for pleasure was immoral. However, the sex instinct is so dynamic that most people could not follow this doctrine, which is being challenged today, even among the pastorate, whose opinions are more inflexible. Masturbation, pre-marital and extra-marital sex are still considered sinful, but a religion's influence is less than it was and many people question its authority to dictate how they run their sexual lives.

The Jewish Reform movement, however, doesn't take a rigid stand on sexuality. Apart from the Orthodox, Jews have fewer inhibitions and prohibitions about sexual behavior than those of other religions. To them it is a personal matter.

Sexuality was a mystery until the advent of Kinsey in the 1950s and Masters and Johnson in the 1960s. Apart from a book by Van de Velde, sexual intercourse was not written or talked about even by doctors, and the Victorian concept dominated the thinking of the population until the end of the nineteenth century when Sigmund Freud opened Pandora's box. A wave of new information about sex washed onto our shores in the 1930s when psychiatrists emigrated from Germany and infiltrated American psychiatric practice, disseminating Freud's theories.

HOW DO WE LEARN ABOUT SEX?

Sound information is hard to come by. There are many books on the subject, but ninety-five percent of what they contain is useless. How do we weed out what applies to us? Asking a doctor is not completely satisfactory, for until twenty years ago, American medical schools did not offer courses in sexology, so most doctors don't have unbiased know-how to discuss and advise on this subject. They only have knowledge of anatomy and personal experience. People go to priests, pastors and rabbis for advice on sex. Why? We look to them for right and wrong, but they don't have the training either.

What about parents? It is the rare parent who makes the overture to instruct a child about sex at any age. It seems almost instinctive for them to protect children from this information and its implications on their lives, and many parents are too embarrassed to broach the subject. Don't the children ask? They ask where babies come from, and are told when a sibling is on the way that the baby is in the mother's "tummy", but don't explain how it got there. Why? There is a hush-hush posture about sex emanating from the Victorian era of a hundred years ago. There is hope, however, for the sexual revolution of the 1960s brought rapid change in people's attitudes and new generations have a freer and more open concept of their sexuality. Unfortunately, this has been less than wisely utilized with sexual license and extremism harming many lives.

The environment can have an influence on sexuality. Either a strict, Puritanical, religious upbringing or a faithless void can create inhibitions, apprehension and even fear, which represses the true expression of sexuality or a lack of self control. But when given the chance and proper education the genuine person will emerge, and time and experience will subtly modify restraints and encourage a healthy fulfillment.

So there are few sources of information on sexuality, for it was poorly studied scientifically until Kinsey and then Masters and Johnson established the Sex Laboratory in St Louis and published data that are proven. However, they don't run an information center and are strictly a research team. They instituted the first required course in sexology at Washington University medical school. Many medical schools now offer this course, but it will be years before the benefits are felt.

PERSONALITY PLAYS A PART IN LOVEMAKING

The thinking person and the doing person differ in how they make love, and there is a gap between thinking and doing in every personality with little feedback between them while making love. Thinking men and women are apt to be inhibited and a strict upbringing makes it worse. They find it difficult to express their feelings, and act as they think they should and not as they want to. They feel guilty about the role they would like to play but are unable to be spontaneous. As these doubts filter through their minds, they wonder what their partners think. They are not really enjoying it and it seems impossible to be natural. A loving nature wants to share affection and love which should go along with intercourse.

The thinking woman becomes involved emotionally and loses her heart to the man with whom she spends the night. Being wanted and possessed casts an aura over her that remains with her throughout the following day. It is a strange and haunting feeling which she holds tightly inside, sharing it with no one. The thinking man is not as analytical or introspective as the woman. He is bent on achieving his climax and striving to hold off until his partner reaches hers. Both would like to reach orgasm together.

The thinking person cannot abide casual sex and a one night stand has no appeal. Doing personalities feel differently. They are extroverted and relaxed about sex, and the environment has little influence on their behavior. They are not concerned about what their partners think, in fact, they are apt to part company with anyone who tries to cramp their style. Some make love with no thoughts at all, following the impulse of the moment.

A doing man can be quite casual about sex, and look for a liaison as need demands. The one night stands are frequent. He has little interest in closeness or stability, and plunges into affairs indiscriminately, without much regard for the feelings of his partner. This causes him to make mistakes in judgment, to which he reacts by "lovin' and leavin'" them.

A doing woman may be available or even promiscuous, but is not as sexually active as a man. Not only is her sex drive lower, but she is looking for a stable relationship, if not marriage, and always has the fear of becoming pregnant. Thus she has deeper feelings about sex and her heart becomes involved, whether or not she wants it to.

How does the average man feel about sex? If he is single, he looks for stimulation from an attractive woman. Once he finds her, he is wary of committing to a relationship, for he is afraid she might ask for more than he is willing to give, such as warmth and affection which few men are capable of. He may also be afraid of being impotent, but this is less of a concern than the fear of not satisfying his partner.

If he is married, he may stray occasionally, not because he doesn't love his wife, but because of his need for sex, a change and a little excitement. He may also have a deep seated wish to get back at her for things she does he finds irritating. As an example, Richard, a physician, is attracted to one of his patients and invited her to work with him. Betty, also married, accepts, and the joint effort set the stage to meet and he persuaded her finally to have an affair. Such a liaison revives the excitement eroded by a long and boring marriage and bolsters the ego. Adolescent impulses return and he is stimulated and refreshed. Then he is ready to go back to the comforts of home, and justifies his actions by rationalizing that it is good for his marriage.

Sex is also a basic need of women. They have as great a capacity for enjoyment as do men, but their drive is less subject to impulse and can be turned off and on. A single woman likes an ongoing relationship with someone with whom she feels comfortable. A tie she can depend upon includes affection as well as sex, and she is willing to give generously and to received little in return. She is glad she is a woman, and experiences a sensation of power in the presence of a man who is attracted to her and she finds attractive. This invisible bond sets off a chain reaction that can lead anywhere, and demonstrates the dominating nature of the sex instinct.

After marriage, a woman is less likely to be unfaithful than is a man. She finds attention and flirtation stimulating, but is apprehensive about having an affair, it is a daring adventure, its outcome unknown. Her husband could find out. She could get pregnant! She doesn't want anything to disturb her marriage, but the temptation is great.

For instance, Janice escaped from the drudgeries of home and children for a short holiday with friends in Canada. A blind date was supplied in Charlie, a widower, older and charming, who fell in love with her. Although she was happy in her marriage, her need for excitement and new stimulation overcame her fears and their discreet affair lasted for several years. Her needs had been fulfilled and eventually her guilt broke off their relationship.

Many women accept advances from men as flattery, in their naiveté and ignorance of the true nature of man's sexual drive. What do we expect of sexuality? What do we want from it? Children? Affection? Flattery? The closeness it personifies? Attention? Power? Possessiveness? Pleasure and excitement? A combination? The key to sexual behavior lies in the answers to these questions and reveals the true and natural sexual self. One woman, when queried, said that sexual intercourse re-establishes the feeling of being a woman and, aside from the physical pleasure, it satisfies her great need for closeness, affection and of being desired.

SEXUAL ATTRACTION

Why are two people attracted to one another? What sparks the awareness of a sexual bond between them? And why is it that sometimes it is one sided? It is difficult to research this phenomenon until we have discovered finely tuned electronic detectors that record the waves of emotion between the brain's sexual center and the body's sex organs. But what triggers it? There are several theories, but none are as yet scientifically proven. However, one is that two people possess biochemical mixtures that are compatible but which may vary in degree, one person sensing greater desire than the other.

According to recent research, the sex hormone testosterone is a powerful aphrodisiac for stimulating sexual desire in both men and women, but more effectively in men. The studies show, however, that there is a vast difference between the biochemistry of desire and that of arousal leading to intercourse. Up until a few years ago, scientists focused on the physiology and emotionality of sexual arousal, and not on desire, which was bypassed mainly for its elusiveness. Today, the emphasis on therapy for all kinds of afflictions, real or imagined, has given rise to sex therapy and studies on desire. Therapists and researchers agree that the matter of sexual desire is an exceptionally complex and many faceted segment of the human condition with a wide range of differences between individuals.

How did they conduct these studies? College students wore a counter on the wrist which they pressed every time they had a thought, a fantasy or the slightest intimation about sex. Some counted over three hundred a day and some experienced hardly any. This study delineates two problems, persons who have little or no sexual desire and the interplay between couples that kills desire for one another when, under different circumstances or with another partners this would not occur. It is gradually becoming known that desire and arousal are disparate processes, influenced by different elements.

The first cause today for seeking sex therapy is a problem with desire. Sex therapists find that thirty-one percent of couples coming for advice complain of the differences in desire between them. Twenty-eight percent complain of too much or too little in one or the other. At this point, research is concerned mostly with the role of testosterone in sexual desire. Although it is considered to be the male sex hormone, probably because it is more plentiful in men and is important in the development of masculinity, women also carry it in smaller quantities. Research shows that testosterone is influential in the promotion of desire, but has no effect on the act of intercourse per se.

It appears that men who have lower than normal levels of testosterone suffer from low levels of desire and, when given testosterone, desire is increased. Sexual fantasies which had ceased to exist are also reinstated. This research and studies by others confirms the fact that testosterone, at least in men, is the prime biological basis of sexual desire. The data in regard to women and testosterone has not been confirmed, although it is found that desire peaks in women half way through the menstrual cycle, when testosterone is at its highest level. In post-menopausal women whose desire is diminished, the administration of testosterone has proved to be successful in reestablishing it.

Emotions and desire are intricately intertwined in both men and women and most couples are aware that anger and emotional upsets between them can lessen sexual desire. It appears that anger plays havoc with desire but does not affect arousal, while anxiety may incite desire but may hinder the act itself. In other words, anxiety provokes desire but decreases the ability to perform, whereas anger devastates desire but does not interfere with the act. So, according to these studies, a conflict between couples restricts their desire more than average levels of stress or anxiety.

Whereas lovemaking is mainly a skill, desire is an emotion, as is anger. When a couple or partner is beset with worries and problems, these may intrude on the ability to become aroused and to make love, but will not necessarily stifle desire.

The experience gleaned by sex therapists regarding the frequency of lovemaking between married couples is erratic, probably because the data were taken from a selected group. Overall, men expressed a greater desire for intercourse more than once a day than women, twelve percent to women's three. After all, their biological need for release is greater and they require a vessel, which most men prefer to masturbation. Four percent of men and ten percent of women desired intercourse once a week, however, the greatest number, forty-two percent of men and fifty percent of women, opted for three or four times.

These figures indicate desire. The actual incidence of sexual intercourse more than once a day was two percent of men and one percent of women, and twelve percent of both sexes enjoyed sex once every two weeks or only once a month.

The level of testosterone in men diminishes after forty years of age, but the desire for intercourse is only slightly less. A sudden lessening seems to be due to other causes such as conflicts in the marriage or boredom with the same partner. However, couples who were married only a few years experienced higher levels of sexual desire than did those married twenty-five years or more, and the levels of desire in post-menopausal women were lower than in younger women.

What else can interfere with sexual desire? Depression is a major target which can be alleviated by the appropriate therapy, and the side effects of some prescription drugs can inhibit desire. It is self-evident that illness and chronic disease can suppress the desire for sexual intercourse.

Today, therapy directed toward problems of sexual desire is concentrated on the quality of the relationship of the couple under treatment. Recent awareness of the interaction of emotions and biochemistry opens up exciting and promising areas of research sex therapists can continue to pursue.

THE INTRICACIES OF LOVEMAKING

Men and women respond in different ways to intercourse, which creates an electric intrigue between them, but if we think "How am I doing?" during love play, it can interrupt natural reactions and cause the failure of one or both partners to reach a climax. So adapting to sex is difficult, more so for a woman because of fear of pregnancy, which can diminish enjoyment except when a child is wanted. While a man has no such threat, sexual intercourse is an intensely emotional experience for him, and he is often equally as concerned as his partner about the possibility of pregnancy.

Although a man's objective is for sexual satisfaction, he also wants his mate to have the same pleasure, and this is not always understood. He takes pride in bringing a woman to orgasm and then achieving his own and is disappointed if she doesn't reach it. The experienced lover blames himself. A man is easily aroused and ready, but it takes longer for a woman, whose motive is different. She craves warmth, affection and security as well as pleasure, and wants her partner to share these too. It is the rare man who can enjoy these same sensations with her, which most women don't realize, so this creates problems in adjusting to mutually satisfying sexual intercourse. Open and frank discussion can resolve these differences.

It takes prolonged fondling to arouse a woman, and she may not understand that this makes it difficult for a man to hold back. He tries to help his partner reach orgasm, but can get so wrapped up in how she is reacting that he becomes tense and may lose his erection.

This upsets the woman, who doesn't realize the interruption was caused by concern for her.

Many men are inept at making love and don't know how to arouse a woman, either because they haven't had the chance to learn or don't see the need for it. Some approach the act with one thought in mind, to obtain relief quickly through ejaculation. They are easily aroused, penetrate and are satisfied within seconds. The woman is left high and dry on the orgasmic plateau, frustrated, and may be annoyed at her partner's disregard for her desire for pleasure also, or blame herself for her inability to maintain his interest.

Some people actually fear intercourse, whether consciously or not. A man is afraid that a woman will dominate or somehow control him, and a woman that the man will take advantage of her or abuse her and cast her aside. This is the paranoid element intruding on what is a natural function. So intercourse is filled with doubt and apprehension that can only be dispelled through experience and candid exchange of feelings, hopes and fears.

The capacity to enjoy lovemaking is inborn and a part of personality and, like any skill, people differ in their ability to make love. We are blessed with a certain degree which can vary from high to low, and we can enhance it, perfect and refine it through experience. Compare it to playing the piano. A person may become a master through long practice, but was born with a talent for it. Conversely, another may have an ardent desire to play well and work very hard, but if there is no inborn talent, he will have less success.

Making love is an art of which few are aware and not many couples venture to work it out together. Lovemaking is complex, with many facets and subtle innuendos, which may relate to one partner and not the other. If one is a connoisseur and the other not so knowledgeable, the denouement is to have a frank and open discussion with no holds barred.

Books have been written on various positions and attitudes that can be applied to lovemaking. No couple tries them all but it is intriguing and challenging to experiment. An experienced lover will lead the way.

There are devices called sex aids which some couples like to use, and they can assist individuals to experience erotic satisfaction while alone. They enhance sexual pleasure and are beneficial for disabled people and those with sexual problems. They come in several forms and are available through the mail or in pharmacies and stores that sell erotica.

There are vibrators used by women to stimulate desire or for couples to massage one another. There is an electrical device called an Accu Jac, shaped like a sleeve, into which a man can place his penis and masturbate to orgasm. A contrivance from the Orient consists of two balls to be placed in the vagina. One is filled with mercury and causes vibrations that stimulate arousal.

There are rings of leather or rubber that fit over the penis and testicles, and can be tightened to help retain an erection, and "French Ticklers" that fit over the penis and tickle the vagina. The surfaces are covered with ridges and flexible points to increase sensation during intercourse. There are creams and lotions of different scents and flavors to rub over the bodies of both partners.

These are some of the sex aids that add to the erotic enhancement of sexual activity for some people. Their use is not considered immoral or derogatory, but both parties should consent when they are used by a couple.

We make love in four stages, the excitement stage in which the man has an erection and the woman is aroused. The plateau stage, when sexual desire increases and the penis enters the vagina. The orgasmic stage after increased stimulation through physical and emotional interaction. The final stage of resolution is the relaxation of both parties. Male orgasm occurs close to a hundred percent of the time and female orgasm less than fifty. Rarely does orgasm occur simultaneously.

Ways of preventing pregnancy are as old as the hills. Some methods are moderately effective, some almost completely. There are contraceptives for women and for men, and more efficient and acceptable methods are being researched and developed. There are devices and there are drugs, some of which are considered a risk to health, and surgery creates sterility in both man and woman. This was irreversible, but new techniques have been developed to reverse these operations.

To prevent pregnancy without a contraceptive, the man may practice "coitus interruptus", that is, withdrawal just before ejaculation. However, a few sperm cells can sneak into the vagina, then it is too late. It takes only one! Another method is to reach orgasm by rubbing against the woman's thighs and ejaculating on the genital area. This gives false security because body warmth helps the sperm cells find their way into the vagina and through the cervical canal to the uterus, whether or not the hymen is still intact. "Virgin" births are known to occur this way. Therefore, neither of these methods is reliable. Never underestimate the vigorous mobility of these tiny organisms and their ability to accomplish their missions.

CONCEPTIONS AND MISCONCEPTIONS ABOUT SEX

Masturbation is self-stimulation of the genitals to orgasm. It is a normal activity of men and women and nature's way of releasing sexual tension. It is not harmful and has no moral implications. Children find the need to masturbate when they first discover the genitals and, as they grow, engage in it privately, boys more frequently than girls.

Women brought up in Victorian ways scold their children when they find them touching their bodies and slap a little boy's hands when he shows interest in his penis. This creates fear associated with the penis, and can be inhibiting in later life. Young men may feel guilty and some are afraid that masturbation causes impotence. Before doctors knew how to treat mental illness, they often blamed it on masturbation Some people still believe that it causes impotence, sterility, acne, and other conditions. It does not. So mistaken beliefs were ingrained through ignorance, resulting in anxiety and anguish.

Is the size of the penis important? No, it is not. A man may be concerned if his is small, but it is much larger in erection. A large penis can be a source of pride, and exciting to some women. Regardless of these differences, the vagina can adjust to a penis of any size. It is also thought that the size varies with the size of the man, but this isn't true. Masters and Johnson discovered that some big men had small penises and vice versa.

Some men believe that circumcision makes the head of the penis more sensitive to stimulation, and some women feel that the uncircumcised penis gives more friction on the clitoris. The Masters and Johnson studies disprove this, and find that circumcision or the lack of it makes no difference in sensations or the ability to prolong erection. Also, if the penis has not been circumcised, the foreskin retracts upon insertion, leaving the head fully exposed.

The clitoris is the subject of much speculation. It is situated at the entrance to the vagina just visible under its hood, and is the center for arousal, acting as the antenna of sexual feelings, both receiving and transmitting. It is, in fact, a tiny penis and answers the same purpose in that it is the first part of the body to respond to mental and manual stimulation, sending sensations of sexual excitement to the brain.

Manipulation of this delicate organ requires gentleness, and once aroused it should be left alone for, as desire builds, it retreats under its hood to await stimulation by the penis, which gives pressure on the hood and the organ itself in preparation for orgasm. Many men mistreat the clitoris with a heavy hand, under the mistaken impression that rubbing it again and again gives pleasure. Heavy stroking may irritate the delicate tissues and interfere with desire, however many women can only achieve orgasm by clitoral stimulation by cunnilingus, to wit, the caressing of the clitoris by her partner's tongue. Some men believe that women release fluid at orgasm as they do. This is not so. However, some women excrete copious amounts of lubricant from tiny glands along the vaginal walls which may give that impression.

ORGASM, THE ULTIMATE GOAL

Orgasm in women is a series of events within the nervous system. A network of nerve fibers contains the trigger point that sets it off. It begins with a spasm of the vaginal walls delivering an overwhelming sensation, than a violent contraction of the uterus and the "pubo-coccygeus" muscle located high in the vaginal vault. Although it has been proved that all women can achieve orgasm, some never do. Many find it difficult to reach the trigger point. There are nerve circuits tied into the network which can interfere, touched off by noises, children nearby, fear, fatigue, preoccupation with the partner, thoughts of previous failure. These distractions make it hard to concentrate and easy to abandon the effort and fake a climax.

On the other hand, there are women who can reach orgasm without effort. For most, however, it depends on the man's ability to prolong ejaculation until they arrive at that trigger point. This can make the difference between pretending and going on to the release which seems so near. A woman can have repeated orgasms, there is no limit. One woman claims that she climaxed twenty-one times and only stopped because of exhaustion. Most women, however, are not interested in having more than one. Some say they cannot remember their orgasms, probably because they have not actually experienced one.

Many women have hysterectomies, and they wonder if orgasm is possible afterwards. The answer is a resounding YES. Surgery does not affect the ability to enjoy sexual relations.

What is the best position for intercourse? Europeans gently disparage the sexuality of Americans by calling the classic position, man on woman, the "American position" and indeed, some couples know no other. However, woman on man is the most advantageous for the woman in reaching orgasm, as it allows her to control stimulation to the clitoris and helps the man withhold ejaculation. There are innumerable positions, however, and a well matched couple can spend much enjoyable time experimenting and inventing a variety of styles and techniques.

Men have conceived theories about female sexuality and years ago they held that there are two kinds of orgasms, clitoral and vaginal. However, research by Masters and Johnson has proved the clitoral orgasm to be false. No doubt this came from the testimony of women who experience sensations about the vagina which they mistake for the real thing, and some women believe this is all there is and stop striving, instead of going on to the overwhelming excitement of a true orgasm. It is an unmistakable sensation, automatic, uncontrollable, wonderful.

At fulfillment, some men and women have an impulsive urge to cry out, losing control. The intensity and quality of the orgasmic cry is individual, and depends on personality. Some cry out with words, some with sound, and others are silent.

There are people who maintain that successful lovemaking must carry both partners to orgasm every time. This is not true. Many women have satisfying and pleasurable sex in spite of infrequent orgasms. Older men need not ejaculate every time they make love. If they don't, it is nature's way of preserving the reduced supply of seminal fluid which occurs with aging.

TRUE FACTS ABOUT IMPOTENCE

What is a "frigid" woman? This means that a woman is unable to enjoy intercourse, and can only be due to outside pressures. This could be one or more of the following: a rigid upbringing, fear of pregnancy, hostility toward her partner, love of another, fear of discovery, restrictions from religious teaching, a transient emotional crisis and so forth. Most reasons can be successfully treated by psychotherapy.

There are millions of men in the United States who suffer impotence, but few know that most cases can be cured. Barring ill health, there is no reason why a man cannot enjoy sexual intercourse well into advanced age. There are two kinds of impotence, psychological and organic. The latter is caused by a physical condition such as illness, surgery, alcoholism, drug abuse, or inadequate blood flow to the penis. Some medications cause impotence. When these causes are ruled out, persistent impotence can come only from a psychological block which, although often obscure in origin, can be diagnosed and treated.

Nature gave man the responsibility for sexual performance, whereas the woman need only to receive the penis. This can create a psychological barrier which prevents erection or causes inability to maintain it. There was no exact definition of impotence until the advent of Masters and Johnson who spelled it out as "the inability to achieve or maintain enough of an erection sufficient to penetrate the vagina at least in four attempts." Until recently, it was estimated that ninety percent of impotence is caused by psychological factors, but in the 1980s, new evidence from research on sleep establishes that normal men experience erections, not associated with erotic dreams, at least five times each night during REM (rapid eye movement) sleep. About fifty percent of impotent men experience these erections during sleep, indicating that a psychological factor is the cause, and the other fifty percent who have no erections suffer from a physical cause.

How does one find out? While there are several more sophisticated methods, a simple device call the "stamp test" is recommended first. A strip of stamps is wrapped around the penis and secured with scotch tape. If, in the morning, the strip is ripped apart along a perforated edge, it is evidence that an erection took place. A band of velcro serves the same purpose. This is repeated for several nights and confirms the diagnosis of psychogenic origin. Many men have been cured of impotence after finding this test positive, which increased confidence and was all that was needed. The next time they made love, they achieved an erection.

The main reason for psychological impotence is fear of the failure to perform which comes from the section of the brain where the sexual drive and its control is located. Every man at some time is unable to have or hold an erection, often for a simple reason, he is overtired, he is not feeling well and so forth. But one failure can create such anxiety that he dwells on it and builds up apprehension. What is wrong? Is he losing his manhood? He has always been able to have an erection! His erection is all he can think about and that he failed for the first time. Is this the beginning of the end of his sex life? This scenario happens all too often and is tragic, for the brain is all important in sexuality.

The height of the male sex drive is around eighteen and slowly diminishes from then on. Most men do not know this and, as they grow older, the gradual decrease in ability to perform builds up a haunting fear. The one thing they fear most is impotence. And the mind plays on the body and the body on the mind and inhibits the sexual response. Impotence ensues. With today's knowledge, this does not have to happen. A man can enjoy sexual intercourse into his eighties and even nineties, barring illness.

What physical conditions cause impotence? The stamp test is sure evidence that if a man has erections during sleep, he can while awake. But if he doesn't have erections, the next step is to find out why by making a diagnosis. Diabetes ranks high on the list and about one half of male diabetics are impotent, because the disease damages the nerves that control erection. Medications account for one out of four cases, such as drugs to control high blood pressure and heart disease. Alcoholism and depression are also culprits and insufficient hormones, injury to the penis and deformities of the sexual organs can also be responsible.

So a correct diagnosis is important. Is there a psychological or a physical problem? If psychological, is it fear or something more obscure? If physical, which of the possibilities are involved? Once the cause is determined, steps are taken to correct it, psychotherapy is initiated for psychological impotence and, for a physical condition, changes in medication, deficiencies in hormones, the treatment of depression, alcoholism and so forth.

There are some disorders that resist treatment, such as diabetes, spinal cord injuries, and brain damage. But most men with these problems can be restored to adequate sexual function by mechanical means. There are several types of prostheses which are applied or surgically implanted that make the flaccid penis rigid for insertion. For a man who faces irreversible impotence and the inability to make love, this is a heaven-sent solution and the restoration of his ego.

MYTHS AND MISCONCEPTIONS ABOUT SEX

Is there a stigma to intercourse during menstruation? Contrary to popular belief, there is no reason, if it is acceptable to both parties. However, it may be repelling to the fastidious. In fact, in the animal world, the only time attraction and copulation takes place is when the female is in heat, for that is when she is fertile. Humans are not fertile during the menstrual period.

Is sex permissible during pregnancy? Desire usually increases in the woman during this time, especially in the early months. Closer to term it may diminish because of fatigue and pressure from the baby, and there may be a risk of premature delivery, so it is wise to consult the physician.

Early in this century, society's concept of a woman's role in sex was tinged with Victorianism. Advice on sex was passed from mother to daughter, and a young bride was told to give in to her husband, but she need not enjoy what he does. She was also told that after the menopause intercourse was considered unnatural and not quite proper, since conception would no longer be possible. There are areas in this country where these notions still prevail!

A woman prefers the right ambiance for making love and puts on a seductive negligee and creates a romantic atmosphere with the lights low and draperies drawn. This instinctive act heightens her feelings of attractiveness and ensures the privacy she needs. It has little effect on most men, however, who are indifferent to what she wears, but indulgent of her preparations.

Both men and women have sensitivities about sex which appear to be instinctive and both respond naturally to them, notwithstanding that what appeals to a man in a woman is quite different than what appeals to a woman in a man, although not necessarily discussed between them. A woman adorns her body in a manner which she presumes appeals to a man, while a man looks through the clothes to what is underneath. Men are more sensitive to touch and visual stimulation and women are more sensitive to words and verbal expressions, although they too may be attracted to an image of manliness. Women consider that attractive clothing that accentuates their bodies are important to men, and that perfume, jewelry, a becoming hair-do and makeup enhances their best features. These adornments may be supportive for her but the man is not enticed by them and would prefer to see her without what he considers superfluous frills and furbelows.

Many believe that a man will lose the ability to have an erection if he doesn't have intercourse regularly. But the saying "Use it or lose it" is false, even if he goes without sex for months. The sexual stimulus is a drive of the central nervous system, however, if a man believes he is impotent and doesn't attempt sex, his fears could cause it to happen, for the mind has a powerful effect on the body. On the other hand, the notion that frequent intercourse depletes strength is also false. Intercourse is a natural function, and the intensity of sex life is determined by energy level, the higher the energy the stronger the sex drive.

SEX AND THE AGING

Do men go through a menopause? It is controversial whether men go through a climacteric between the ages of forty-five and sixty-five, but there is no way of proving this one way or the other. There are few changes in hormonal balance, the most noticeable physical change being balding. Psychological changes are more subtle. Communication between husband and wife deteriorates, bringing misunderstandings about sex and a decrease in sexual activity. The man experiences mood swings, is anxious about losing his sex drive, and is tempted to look elsewhere for proof of his manhood. The woman may doubt her ability to attract her husband and loses interest in sex. Occasionally, she may decline to have intercourse and encourages her husband to find someone else. All of this puts a strain on their relationship which may be already rooted in other areas, such as financial insecurity.

Linked to the male sex drive is the urge for sexual excitement and the desire for new sensations. As human instincts are closely related to those of animals, an interesting theory on the polygamous nature of man was recently inferred from research on their sexual strategies. Since the sex drive is directed toward survival of the species, male animals mate with as many females as possible. Scientists at Oxford, England and the University of California at Santa Barbara theorize that man inherits this tendency from his sex instinct, which explains the conflict between fidelity and the lure of the new.

The menopause in women occurs when the ovaries no longer produce eggs and regular menstruation comes to an end. This takes place between the ages of forty-five and sixty-five, the average being fifty-one. Some women call it the beginning of old age, others welcome it as freedom from the fear of pregnancy and the nuisance of menstruation. For most, the menopause opens up a new and exciting phase of sexuality, for some, interest is rekindled or enhanced, in others it is diminished or lost.

Is sex possible after sixty? Most definitely. Recent studies show that the majority of sexually active people continue well into their sixties and seventies and, as noted earlier, Masters and Johnson proved that a man can perform for as long as he retains his health. Men are known to have fathered babies in their eighties and nineties. As for women, many become more interested in sex and more proficient at lovemaking after the menopause.

For reasons not understood, society is reticent about discussing sexuality between aging persons, and it is accepted by many that to have sex after a certain age is "just not done". That "certain age" is not defined and differs from person to person, but around sixty appears to be the popular time. This tenet is a total misconception, for there is no valid reason why men and women cannot enjoy their sexuality as long as they wish.

Does a man's sexual function change? Of course, the body slows down with age, and sexual ability slows down too. It takes longer to reach erection and to achieve it again after orgasm. A definite plus, however, is the increased ability to control the urge to ejaculate which affords opportunity to try new positions and techniques, and is beneficial for the woman who usually needs more time. Aging may cause difficulty at times in acquiring an erection and a man may panic that he is finished. Fear compounds the problem and he accepts the inevitable. But many men have been restored to active sexual function through counseling and, barring illness or real abuse of the body, they can continue pleasurable sexual relations.

There are four changes that occur in a man's sexual functioning as he approaches sixty. First, it takes him longer to achieve full erection, and often he may need stimulation by his partner and by him. Second, there is a decrease in the amount of seminal fluid in his ejaculate and the force by which it is expelled.

The third and perhaps most distressing change is his inability to ejaculate on demand even though deeply aroused. This may occur during one out of three or four episodes. Some men never experience this, and some to an excessive or a lesser degree, but it can be very disturbing. It is a natural phenomenon and no cause for concern. It is nature's way of conserving the diminishing amount of seminal fluid a man is able to produce. The fourth change is that some men find it difficult to attain or maintain an erection. This is perfectly normal in the aging male, but he fears that he has lost his manhood. His first failure is permanent and he is condemned to celibacy. But don't give up, for many men have been restored to active sexual function through counseling.

One or more of these signs can produce in a man the fear of impotence and cause his partner to feel insecure in her ability to attract her mate or that he is expending his sexual energy elsewhere. This further augments the lack of communication concerning sex and results in harm to the relationship.

Changes also occur in the sexual performance of a woman as she ages. After the menopause, the vaginal walls become thin and lubrication diminishes due to the reduction of estrogen, the female hormone. This results in pain on penetration and is avoided by use of a lubricating cream. When a woman goes without sex for a long time, a condition called vaginismus may set in. This is a constriction of the lower part of the vagina resulting in painful intercourse, often causing her to make excuses not to participate. Some women experience cramps in the lower abdomen during orgasm, which may discourage intercourse or the desire to reach orgasm. However, this is rare.

All of these conditions are produced by the loss of estrogen which causes the thinning of the walls of the vagina and the reduction of lubrication. The gynecologist can remedy them by prescribing estrogen and exercises.

There are three criteria for maintaining a satisfactory sexual liaison. First, the good health of both parties, then, a sound relationship, and third, the mutual ability to communicate the intimacies of lovemaking. A long marriage, no matter how stable, is sometimes beset by boredom with the sex act, which can accumulate to such an extent that it negates the pleasure, and lovemaking is gradually abandoned.

It is generally agreed that as they age, both men and women require more time for foreplay in order to reach the optimal level of desire. This is especially true of women, who have always taken more time, which may be construed as an excuse to forgo intercourse, but the pleasure a woman derives from sex remains as strong as ever. It never leaves her.

Granted that older people don't have as great an interest or enjoy sex as much as they did at twenty-five, but they never outgrow their sexuality or the desire for physical intimacy. It may not be as exciting or as emotionally obsessive, nevertheless, it can be loving and affectionate and endearing. A sexual relationship must be nurtured with tender loving care, no matter what the age of the participants, but especially during aging. Thus, each can give to the other joy and fulfillment.

Society has failed older people by imposing conditions to which they are supposed to adhere in regard to sexual performance. Although the Victorian and Puritan eras have passed and the sexual revolution is no fledgling, society has neglected to address the sexual conduct of those who are aging and whose numbers are growing. They have as much right as the young to enjoy the pleasures of their sexuality, and with the burgeoning advances in the prevention and treatment of disease, they promise to increase many fold.

WHAT ARE SEXUAL VARIATIONS?

The terms "variation" and "deviation" are used interchangeably. We prefer variation and use it for any sexual activity other than genital to genital intercourse between a man and a woman. Variations include cunnilingus, fellatio, fondling, masturbation and all forms of body touch. Cunnilingus is the manipulation of the clitoris by the man with his tongue, sometimes to orgasm of the woman. Fellatio is when the woman sucks the penis; the man may ejaculate into her mouth. Some women take pleasure in this but to others it is repugnant. These sentiments should be conveyed and mutually agreed upon, as well as all approaches to and techniques in lovemaking. Only thus can ways of giving and sharing love and ecstasy be enjoyed by both parties. When agreed upon, these practices are not pathological, even when the love play does not end in intercourse. Sexual perversions, on the other hand, are pathological, or sick and unhealthy. These are described later.

Sadism is a variation. The word comes from the name of the Marquis de Sade, an eighteenth century French nobleman, who wrote about his practice of abusing women for sexual pleasure. Today, it means the infliction of pain as a means of sexual satisfaction. Both men and women play this role to some degree, and it is not uncommon for lovers to bite or scratch one another in the heat of passion, but is considered a perversion when used as the only means of obtaining orgasm.

Through the years, sadism has taken on the broader meaning of the urge to hurt someone who is envied, disliked or unattainable. The forms it takes are limitless, ranging from vicious gossip and cruel sarcasm to open hostility and physical torture. Sadists take pleasure watching the results of their attacks and seeing their victims suffer. The urge for retribution toward someone who has wronged us is a mild form of sadism. We all harbor a twinge in our psyches.

Masochism, a counterpart of sadism, is submissive and feminine, sadism is aggressive and masculine. The word is derived from the name of a nineteenth century Austrian novelist, Leopold von Sacher-Masoch, whose autobiography portrayed women as cruel and men as weaklings. He had known cruelty as a child and associated sexual excitement with submissiveness and pain, mirroring his experiences. His writings helped his concept of pain as pleasure, related to sex specifically and an urge to be hurt generally.

The tendency to find sexual pleasure in self-deprivation, submissiveness and humiliation is a mild version of masochism, and translates as sadism when applied to another person. These traits appear in both sexes and cover all gradations of emotional feeling and expression, from the pleasure and pain of the average individual to the gross, pathological manifestations of the hardened criminal.

Masochism takes many forms: social, verbal, moral, mental and physical. All involve gratification through pain. It enters the sexual arena when a person reaches orgasm through the infliction of pain. A masochist may enjoy injuring himself, or if he is injured, sick or hurt, would rather suffer than seek medical care.

"Playing the martyr" is a mild form of masochism, such as a person denying himself a pleasurable experience, like staying home moping, rather than going to the party. This is the passive quality of masochism. The masochist takes pleasure in degrading himself verbally, especially to someone for whom he has little regard. An example of benign masochism is the hen-pecked husband, who seems to enjoy being ordered around by his wife. Sadism and masochism are so closely associated that the term sado-masochism has come into use. Many of those afflicted with one condition show symptoms of the other.

Narcissism is the face in the mirror. It is described in Greek mythology. The nymphs with whom Zeus philandered tried to hide his infidelities from Hera, his wife, and assigned one of them, Echo, to hold Hera's attention by chattering to her incessantly. Hera was not fooled, and punished Echo by not allowing her to speak unless spoken to. Disheartened, Echo fell in love with Narcissus, the handsome son of a river god, who rejected her. This angered the gods and they punished him by making him so enamoured of his own reflection in the water that he pined away and turned into the flower that bears his name.

Are there narcissists today? Yes, both men and women are. It is best described as egocentrism and, in an inordinate amount, it is unhealthy. An excessive narcissist is extremely self-centered and expects favors without giving anything in return. He is totally dependent on the attention and admiration of others. He is unable to love another, and has little use for people except as admirers. While this seems like self-love, the opposite is true. Narcissists hate themselves and have such low self-esteem they must look for approval in order to build it up. When criticized, they react with anger or indifference, but are quick at using others for their own gain.

Narcissists are exhibitionists and have fantasies of power, beauty, success and ideal love. Most are sexually promiscuous and make advances to those who are especially desirable, attractive or valuable to know, including the most unattainable. Such people excite them sexually but they soon lose interest and move on to what they think are greener fields.

There is a smidgen of narcissism in all of us, and it takes many forms, almost always with sexual implications. It is an ingredient of emotional immaturity, however, it shows up in mature personalities in a healthy manner in those who are well groomed and keep themselves in good physical condition. If you are a woman, do you dress for men, other women or yourself? If you are a man, for whom do you groom yourself? for your boss? For women? For yourself? Each person is individual and has his or her goals, depending on personality, and the degree of the narcissistic characteristic we all have.

WHAT IS AN APHRODISIAC?

An aphrodisiac is a substance that stimulates sexual arousal. The word comes from Aphrodite, the Greek goddess of love and beauty. Apples are not considered an aphrodisiac today, but when Eve offered Adam one, it did the trick. It seems that ever since then, men and women have been looking for foods to kindle the sexual passion of one on whom they have set their hearts. Ancient Greeks recommended that newlyweds take honey during the waxing and waning of the first moon of their married life. Hence the honeymoon. In Rome it was herbs, in seventeenth century Europe, chocolate; coffee was tried and believed to be working, but finally abandoned. In the Far East, ginseng was used and is still considered an enhancer of sexual performance.

Some drugs are said to have these properties, such as hashish, cantharides, blatta orientalis, and damiana, all extracted from tropical plants and all harmful with habitual use. The Old Testament mentions mandrake root, and Oriental literature offers birds' nest soup. Arabian sheiks consumed large quantities of milk, eggs, honey, nuts, seeds and garlic to help them take care of their harems.

So the search continues for the perfect aphrodisiac, so far without success, and contrary to popular belief, we know of none that is used universally and safely. Today, the sale of and over the counter substance with the claim of arousing sexual passion is illegal, only an occasional prescription drug is available and it is questionable as to its effectiveness.

An aphrodisiac is also an experience of the senses that arouses sexual desire, such as smell or touch or sight. For a man, this can be a woman's perfume, the scent of her hair or body or the smell of a flower that has romantic associations. The sight of a beautiful woman, her breast or legs or buttocks can arouse some men.

For a woman, it is the physical attributes that attract, as she meets or confronts a man. She is conscious of the manhood he personifies, his looks, how he comes across, his approach, the personality he projects. Immediately, she senses, as though by instinct and with undeniable certainty, that the attraction is reciprocated.

In the case of both men and women, the deciding factor is the compatibility of the biochemical makeup of the individual who attracts. This is an unfathomable element and never has been studied scientifically. These experiences can occur daily, depending on the opportunity to mingle with others. Although mutual attraction may occur fairly often, most pass like ships in the night. Only occasionally does a chance meeting evolve into a communal relationship.

MORE VARIATIONS OF SEXUALITY

Nymphomania is not abnormal, nor is it an illness. The word simply means a high sex drive. Research shows that extreme sexual arousal is natural in vigorous, highly sexed women, fulfilled by frequent sexual activity. If this occurs, however, in a woman who is not highly sexed, it may be an indication of the need for attention and support.

Transvestism means literally "cross dressing". It is the impulse to dress in the clothing of the opposite sex in order to derive sexual satisfaction. In some cases, a man may take an article of his wife's or lover's underclothing and touch his genitals. This is a stimulant to arousal and is usually a prelude to intercourse or, more often, to masturbation.

Transvestism is a genetic trait that remains throughout life. It is rare and extremely rare in women. It is a recessive gene that crops up with no known family history. It's a wiring defect in the brain whereby the stimulation that usually comes from a woman or a man comes from that person's clothes. It is not serious and should be accepted as a minor sexual variation with no harmful effects. It seldom presents a problem except when there are feelings of guilt or disapproval through lack of understanding by the spouse.

If the wife of a thinking person treats her husband with understanding and cooperation, it minimizes his guilt. The doing person can take the situation in stride, as he is less self-critical. When a transvestite's wife is primarily a thinker, she is likely to be upset if she finds her husband draped in her clothing. This can be threatening to her and counseling may be necessary. The woman who is more of a doer is likely to sympathize, cooperate and make it easy for her husband. Transvestism is pathologic only when it becomes the principal means of sexual gratification.

Transvestites are normal, heterosexual males who marry, have children, and make good husbands and fathers. The transvestite woman is also heterosexual, but has a lower sex drive than most women. If the tendency is extreme, a man may be deeply ashamed and try to resist it. He doesn't want to be a woman, only to give in to his compulsion occasionally. Then he dresses behind closed doors in feminine apparel such as pantyhose, underwear, a wig and lipstick. This arouses him to a degree he can reach no other way, and allows him to be more passionate with his wife. Often he is stimulated to masturbate.

Transvestism can become a problem when a predominantly thinking man becomes obsessed with shame and guilt to such an extent he falls into depression. Such a man is conscientious, well organized, upright and intelligent, and anxiety can make him imagine that others know of his "weakness". He may even leave a good position under this false impression.

It is difficult for the adolescent transvestite, whose sex drive is at its height. He experiences an uncontrollable urge, and usually steals clothing from his mother, sister or a girl friend. If his mother finds out and scolds him, he is still compelled to obtain what he needs and may end up in trouble. Counseling can help him and his family understand and accept his habit as harmless and a legitimate outlet for his sex drive. He can be shown how to avoid exposure and reassured that he is not a homosexual, which he may fear.

Homosexuals are not transvestites, although they are as prone to inherit the gene as the heterosexual. Some people contend that only homosexuals are transvestites, because some dress in women's clothing, or "drag". The transvestite uses it for sexual stimulation, while homosexuals wear "drag" to indicate that they are playing the female role, the "queen".

Fetishism is another minor variation and is almost non-existent in women. It is similar to transvestism in that attention is focused on an article belonging to the opposite sex. However, the fetishist regards it as a symbolic love object and idolizes it from a distance rather than by contact. It is a perfectly harmless aberration and everyone has a trace. Most women enjoy washing and taking care of their husbands' and children's clothes, folding them and putting them away. Men delight in giving pretty things to their wives and loved ones. Both men and women like to buy for those they love. It gives them a moment of pleasure and brings up their images.

This condition is pathologic when a man is sexually aroused only by using a fetish. He discards it afterwards, and may have to steal to replace it, for he requires a new one each time. There are extreme cases when a man is deprived of sex or unsure of his sexual adequacy, becomes infatuated with a woman beyond his reach and attains sexual satisfaction with a fetish. In such an instance, fetishism is almost indistinguishable from transvestism. Both variations lower self-esteem and interfere with personal relationships. Psychotherapy can help.

AN UNUSUAL WOMAN

Many homosexual men marry, and one wonders what type of woman marries them. Usually they are passive, lonely, timid gals with a low sex drive, or the unusual woman described here who is powerfully attracted to the aesthetic type of man often personified in the homosexual. She is willing to put up with considerable mistreatment and often rejection, and although she presents a mannish appearance, she is heterosexual. She has a complex personality which includes a tendency to be cruel to other women and difficulty in getting along with people. She is not overly fond of children and if she has them, is apt to resent them.

How does she get her man? A gay man marries either for money, social advantage or to hide his homosexuality. The bisexual often falls in love. If at a young age, when his sex drive is high, this allows him to channel some into his marriage, at least for a time. Such a marriage, however, doesn't last, and by middle life he may go off with a male lover. His wife usually tries to find another homosexual man of the same type.

This unusual woman is an intense person who is sexually excited by a man who rejects heterosexual relations, so the sexual bond is distorted. Homosexuals prefer oral and anal sex and usually demand that their wives engage in these practices. Her desire is so strong, however, that she cooperates with his preference to the exclusion of a fulfilling love life for her. Although they sometimes have children, they avoid vaginal sex, because this presents emotional difficulties for the husband.

Is a gay man as stimulated by a woman as by a man when engaging in oral or anal sex? This question remains unanswered due to scarcity of data, but experienced professionals agree that homosexual men are not aroused by anything a woman does, and that this becomes more marked with age.

The woman who marries a homosexual must accept that he will be an inadequate husband in many respects, not only sexually. Homosexuals present the worst characteristics of males and females, combining aggressiveness and bitchiness, and can be very unpleasant when challenged. Some make adequate fathers, but most lack real feelings for their wives, who serve only to close gaps in their lives. The woman who loves a homosexual will continue to grieve about his infidelities and his lack of love for her. This he is incapable of doing, but she never accepts it.

This unusual woman's family background falls into a classic pattern. Her mother is extremely paranoid and uninterested in children. She makes a poor mother and more often than not has only one. The father is a passive, well-meaning man, artistic and sensitive, who allows his wife to rule the household. His personality lets him bend to his wife's demands, ensuring peace in the household. So this woman has a unique combination of personality traits, some of which are genetic.

INCEST IS NEWS TODAY

Just what is it? Incest is sexual activity between members of a family related by blood or marriage. It may be caressing and fondling, oral sex, masturbation, intercourse. The most frequent act is between siblings and is the least reported. The next is between mother and son. The most frequently reported is a father with his daughter. Homosexual relationships also exist, i.e. father/son, mother/daughter. It is estimated that between ten and twenty million people in the United States from all socioeconomic levels are or have been involved in incest.

Father/daughter incest usually begins as the child reaches puberty, or after she starts to menstruate. It may occur earlier and represent the only affection given by that parent. It happens with teenage daughters as well, but girls are better able at that age to reject overtures by their fathers. For example, in a father/daughter involvement, the girl may see herself in competition with her mother, and the father might treat her with special attention, neglecting the other children. The wife may be angry or jealous if she suspects what is going on, or even condone the affair, having lost desire for her husband, and grateful for having been relieved of what she considers her obligation. If she is unaware, she may question her husband's attitude toward that daughter.

Whether or not the relationship comes to an end, the emotional disruption of the family continues and can even cause divorce.

Incestuous acts usually take place over a period of time, seldom only once. Physical force is rarely used, but persuasion by emotional and psychological methods predominate. The relationship is usually initiated by the parent, seldom the child. Incest is not well studied, but there is evidence that it is more prevalent than is reported. This is probably due to the taboo that exists which is universal in all cultures. Although matters of sex are discussed freely today, incest is still an unmentionable.

What kind of man has incest with his daughter? There are no studies on this, the only data are on men imprisoned for incest, which hardly represents a true profile of the personality. Many of these men come from emotionally deprived and low economic backgrounds, and the consensus is that they are passive and dependent and cannot deal maturely with other adults, particularly women, and lack self-esteem and self-confidence.

Furthermore, a consistent pattern of alcoholism or drug abuse is apparent and evidence of a personality disorder. They are hard working and well behaved men, but have poor interpersonal relations with their families, particularly their wives. They all admit in therapy that the sexual outlet with their children was wrong, but this did not deter them. Such psychopathic thinking is typical of the excessive doing personality, when the doing speaks louder than the thinking, overriding the conscience.

So it is the more doing type who has sexual intercourse with his daughter, without thought as to what it might do to her, and as personality traits are inherited, the chances are that she is also more of a doer. This accounts for the long-term character of an unnatural relationship. A more thinking daughter might be forced into it by threats, but is loath to maintain the liaison and blows the whistle.

Are these relationships damaging? Yes. They are psychologically detrimental to both parties. Sometimes the child is physically hurt, some are emotionally affected for life, others for a short time, depending on the personality. A relationship of mother and son is particularly destructive to the son. In all instances, both the child and the adult carry guilt feelings for a long time, often for life.

One of the most disastrous consequences of incest is the effect on the entire family. The roles of its members are confused, and normal relationships of husband and wife, parent and child and siblings are greatly influenced and enormously distorted while incest is taking place and after it is discovered. Thoughts of incest turn us off, but the time comes when, for no apparent reason, they creep into consciousness. We may visualize our parents in bed, or think about intercourse with a sister or brother. Perhaps this never happens but when it does, we are repelled and quickly close our minds. Why? Because we have a strong taboo within us that sets up a mental block.

This taboo is one of our instincts. It evolved in man to ensure healthy children and the continuity of the family, for it is well known that the offspring of closely related parents often are born with serious conditions like mental retardation or malformations. A classic example is the inbreeding practiced by the Egyptian pharaohs in the belief that they were preserving the royal strain. Brothers and sisters, fathers and daughters, mothers and sons intermarried. In fact, the royal family was forbidden to marry outside, although there were many illegitimate children. This intensive inbreeding increased the incidence of undesirable genes which were passed on until the line was destroyed.

What leads to incestuous activity? Incest is a symptom of conflict within the person or the family. Marital discord can turn a man to his daughter for the warmth and approval he doesn't receive from his wife, an unsatisfactory relationship between mother and daughter can precipitate incest between father and daughter, and a household that is disorganized and undisciplined plays a role in creating unnatural alliances. Overcrowding is a contributing factor coupled with the strong male sex drive and the unavailability of normal sexual affiliations. Alcoholism and drugs are another force that releases inhibitions and reduces good judgment.

Sibling incest can result from social isolation, poor personality development and ineffectual, passive parents, who give no guidance or set examples. And sibling incest can result from exploring one another's bodies when young which continues as the children reach adolescence.

Can incest be treated? Yes, but it takes many services. Psychiatric, psychological and medical assessment is needed for in-depth evaluation of the entire family. Individual psychotherapy, group and family therapy are helpful, and self-help groups for adolescents are also. And there are residential programs for young people who cannot or will not accept discipline or discipline themselves.

Is there punishment for incest? Yes, a father faces criminal action if he has sexual intercourse with his daughter. He also risks humiliation and the break-up of the home. There is no legal action against other forms, i.e., sibling, mother/son and so forth. If a boy is involved in mother/son incest, he has a difficult time developing a full emotional life. He may be unable to relate to girls and women, and establish relationships leading to marriage. He has extreme guilt feelings and may suffer from anxiety and depression for a long time. Such experience is very hard on a boy, especially if he is more of a thinker. The doer is less affected.

A girl is especially vulnerable to the effects of an incestuous relationship, which is usually with her father or stepfather. Although it may last for years, why doesn't she break it off? It may be the fear of reprisal or the reluctance to disobey her parent and, conversely, a feeling of superiority over her siblings and peers, whom she surmises have no sexual experience. Or she may crave warmth and affection she lacks from elsewhere. As she matures, she may find that she derives pleasure in sex and would like it to continue. In this event, the notion that the liaison is illicit plays no part.

However, at the same time, a girl has diminished self-image with guilt feelings and anger toward her family for not protecting her. If she is a more thinking person, she may feel dirty and become depressed. Such an association can result in difficulty establishing satisfying relationships with men in the future, so she ends up with a series of casual alliances, and problems with arousal and orgasm. The girl with a more doing personality survives incest with less trauma.

An incestuous act usually takes place over a period of time with the child submitting and even taking an active role, but it is the child, however, who eventually blows the whistle. Fortunately, few babies are born from incest and we don't know why. If a child does result, he or she may be intelligent and healthy, mentally deficient or have a severe physical defect. It is well known that inbreeding results in congenital malformations, as demonstrated by the Egyptian Pharaohs and Greek and Roman nobility.

All in all, incestuous acts are more harmful to the child than the adult, both emotionally and psychologically, although many adults, especially the thinking kind, are gravely affected.

A BIT OF HISTORY

While incest was condoned in Greek, Egyptian and Roman cultures, Mosaic law as set forth in the old Testament exacted severe punishment for incest, exhibitionism and voyeurism. (Gen. 9:20-22) "And the man that lieth with his father's wife hath uncovered his father's nakedness; both of them shall surely be put to death; their blood shall be upon them. And if a man shall take his sister, and see her nakedness, it is a wicked thing; and they shall be cut off in the sight of their people, he hath uncovered his sister's nakedness; he shall bear his iniquity. And if a man shall lie with his uncle's wife, he hath uncovered his uncle's nakedness; they shall bear their sin; they shall die childless. And if a man shall take his brother's wife, it is an unclean thing; he hath uncovered his brother's nakedness; they shall be childless."

Another passage from the Old Testament tells of a widower and his two daughters who lived in a cave in the country and had no social contacts because of their isolation. Both women desperately wanted children, so they persuaded their father to drink a good deal of wine, and manipulated him into sexual relations. They both became pregnant and bore the babies they yearned for. The role of women in those days was to bear children, not to have them was to fail. The act of the daughters is justified, therefore, and the father is excused as being unaccountable for what he did, having been plied with wine.

7

ANOTHER KIND OF SEXUALITY

We have just discussed "heterosexuality," or sexual activity between a man and a woman. There is another kind, "homosexuality" which in some men and women is a variation of sexuality when the sex drive is directed toward someone of the same sex. A person may be partially or totally homosexual, and there are many degrees. When partial, it is called bisexual, meaning a man or woman can be attracted to both sexes. In all variations, hormonal function is often as normal as in heterosexuals. It is not more estrogens in males and more androgens in lesbians, i.e., the sex hormones. The difference is in the response of the brain to the hormones.

Homosexuals are a minority group, comprising about ten percent of the population, and have been with us since the evolvement of the human race. Some people consider them abnormal and some think homosexuality is an illness. Some condemn them as immoral and wrong and to be despised. It is none of these things.

Throughout history, homosexuals have been subjected to judgment ranging from total acceptance to total rejection. For example, the American Plains Indians considered male homosexuals valuable members of the household and the community. Families adopted them to do the work of a woman with a man's strength, and there is no record of rejection by the braves.

In ancient Greece and Rome, homosexuals were not considered a threat. They were accepted and commingled freely. There was a high rate of homosexual activity in both societies and men bought and sold young boys to satisfy their needs. Hero and Caligula, both Ceasars, were homosexual, and male prostitutes were numerous and accepted by society. Since that time, homosexuals have not enjoyed this liberality, for around 300 A.D., laws were enacted banning the practice of homosexuality, and anal intercourse was punishable by death. From then on matters became more difficult for homosexuals, especially as Christianity became widespread.

By the eleventh century, the Catholic church punished homosexual priests and monks severely and by 1600, they were punished in England by having their goods and land taken and in some instances by death. By the beginning of the nineteenth century, Napoleon relaxed the laws in France and homosexual acts between consenting adults were condoned, but England and the United States remained adamant and reinforced them. By this time, the laws in most countries were directed against the male homosexual and lesbianism was regarded as not existing.

Today, the United States continues to have repressive laws about homosexuality, while many western countries have relaxed them, including England, France, Holland, Italy, Spain, the Scandinavian countries and several in South America. In the U.S. being homosexual is not illegal, but performing or solicitating sexual acts with a member of the same sex is.

In the United States, the states differ in respect to the laws, but most adhere to sodomy and soliciting favors as misdemeanors or felonies. In addition, both men and women homosexuals are denied civil rights in housing and employment. They are discriminated against in credit, insurance, and child custody and neither have the privilege of marrying and receiving the tax and legal benefits, or property and inheritance rights associated with legally sanctioned unions.

How did this discrimination against homosexuals happen? Judeo-Christian teachings are from the Bible and religious leaders and scholars have interpreted them. Actually, the scriptures relate the practices of homosexuality per se, and not individuals with homosexual orientation, as evil and contrary to the will of God, and only males are mentioned, females only in passing. The interpretation of the scriptures by the hierarchy connotes otherwise and has resulted in the condemnation by many people of gay men and women.

During the past fifteen years, religious groups are beginning to slacken their hold on the rights and wrongs of homosexuality. The conservative and reformed groups of Judaism are accepting homosexuals with compassion and understanding, although still adhering to the fundamental writings of the Talmud.

Several Protestant groups are relenting in their opinion of homosexuals and a few accept their civil rights, even to including them as worthy of receiving the privileges offered by the church and the community at large.

It is admitted by members of most religious denominations that there are many homosexual men active and working within the church and serving the community with no questions asked. Nevertheless, the Catholic church remains unyielding in its disapproval and censure of homosexuality in any form.

What makes a homosexual? Homosexuality is genetic or congenital, or a combination of the two. We are not sure which factor or how much of each is involved. Genetic implies a defective gene, present from conception. Mental retardation, Down's syndrome and hemophilia are examples, and are defects of a gene of one of the parents, ordained when the sperm penetrated the ovum. Congenital means that some influence during the baby's development within the uterus interfered with normal formation. A cleft palate (hare lip) and dislocation of the hip are examples.

There is a natural incidence in the population of male and female homosexuals and nothing that happens during puberty or adolescence can prevent or change it. Those infants are stamped for life at birth with a brand of sexuality that is irreversible by the parents, the family, the environment, training, peer pressure or any other factor including the individual him or herself. Sexual preference, whether hetero- or homosexual is derived from a prearranged direction set in the baby's brain while in the uterus, triggered off at puberty, but usually evident earlier by behavior.

The theory that homosexuality is a product of the environment is still widely held. It was firmly established in professional and lay minds in the late nineteenth century, and it was believed that young boys could be made into homosexuals by their mothers, or by men or other boys. These concepts were formed from insufficient evidence, reinforced by superstition and pseudo science. It is still true today, that some psychiatrists claim heredity plays no part and that the environment or the mother can produce it and psychotherapy can remove it. None of this has been proved.

These beliefs were discredited by an extensive research project conducted at the Kinsey Institute for Sex Research at Indiana University. Fifteen hundred male and female homosexuals were interviewed after filling out a lengthy questionnaire. They testified that the parents had nothing to do with their sexual orientation and not one had become homosexual after a homosexual experience. It may be alleged that memories of childhood can be faulty, but until genetic engineering discovers the gene responsible, there is no research that challenges this study.

One conclusion of the Kinsey report is that homosexual boys have unsatisfactory relationships with their fathers, if they tend to be overbearing, controlling, cold, hostile and lacking of understanding, the typical paranoid personality. Several psychiatrists have observed this over years of practice and, while still theoretical, it suggests a genetic influence on the fetus. The personality of the mother is less influential and little is known about her genetic or congenital effect. Experiments with animals, however, show that male homosexual activity shows up when the mother's hormonal balance is thrown off by adding male hormones. There is need for further study in this area.

Most homosexuals are comfortable in their roles and are mature, happy, and well adjusted to life, although they are subject to mood swings and anxiety. According to the Kinsey researchers, most don't go to psychiatrists for advice, but those who do, go for reasons other than sexual preference. However, because of the enormous pressure that is put on them by family, church, friends, many gays end up seeking some means of changing their sexual identity "to be cured". This is unfortunate, for the emotional and psychological havoc that such a program produces is devastating beyond description. Those gays who have asked to have their sexual orientation changed as a last desperate grab for acceptance by the straight world, have without exception come to deeply regret that decision. This pressure by society to force gays to change puts a burden on them that has never been visited upon straights and can wreak irreparable damage.

The word "cure" implies sickness and to be homosexual is not to be sick. And gays have grown up and remain surrounded by a culture that regards homosexuality as sick or worse, a wicked way to be and against God's will. These concepts are absolutely false. As already explained, homosexuality occurs naturally in a certain percentage of male and female individuals through factors of genetic and/or congenital nature, and is irreversible. This has been true of mankind since recorded history. The exact cause or causes still remain unknown.

Moreover, it appears to be accepted that compassion for a gay person by a straight is manifested in a desire and an effort to change him or her. Few straights either don't know or will not admit that this is not possible, and persist in efforts to persuade gays to change. Some people are under the mistaken impression that gays are trying to convert straights to homosexuality. This is not true. It is the other way around.

"Change" or "cure" programs are referred to by Masters and Johnson as "conversion" or "reversion" treatment and were sought out by both gay men and lesbians, more men than women. The degree of motivation of the client was important in evaluating the method of treatment and the chance of success. While a relatively few homosexuals asked to have their sexual orientation changed, the motivating reason of all was because of societal and business pressures and rejection. None expressed a real desire. The term conversion applies to men and women who have never had a heterosexual experience, and reversion to those who had or were married and less and less able to have sexual intercourse with their wives or husbands.

There were fifty-four men treated with a partner of the opposite sex of which, nine were totally homosexual requesting conversion, the rest reversion. Each case was studied thoroughly and the treatment outlined individually and altered along the way as circumstances warranted. The results of the treatment were mixed. Some returned to homosexuality, some became or remained ambivalent, and most decided for reversion or conversion and maintained their commitment over the ten years after treatment when they were followed up. Eleven men and three women failed the treatment. Sixteen men and three women were lost to follow-up, the overall failure rate was 28%.

The devastating depression that ensues after an attempt at conversion or reversion that is not successful, and most are not, is tragic to observe and extremely difficult to treat. The only therapy for such a depression is intensive psychotherapy.

There are three kinds of homosexuality, one exclusively homosexual, another bisexual, and a small group recently identified by Masters and Johnson as "ambisexual". The bisexual may marry and have children, the ambisexual enjoys sexual relations with anyone who responds to him or her and is equally comfortable with a partner of either sex.

Homosexuals cannot be identified with any confidence. Superficial features, like mannerisms, posturings, and clothing are not necessarily indicative, nor is the voice, body movement or appearance. They are offended by being pointed out on this basis. In fact, physical traits that are considered homosexual are noticeable in only fifteen percent of males and five percent of females.

Homosexuals are becoming more overt in behavior as society accepts them. Much is natural, but some put it on to attract partners or to challenge society. Some flaunt a supercilious, antagonistic style, characteristic of their worst features, the aggressiveness of the male and the bitchiness of the female. The men are often the ectomorphic type, tall and slight of build, less often of the mesomorphic, muscular build. They may have feminine characteristics and mannerisms and are usually artistic, preferring occupations that call for creativity. The women are most often masculine in appearance and have male mannerisms and gestures. The term for such women is "dyke".

Male homosexuals enjoy one another, using many sexual techniques, with the objective of orgasm and ejaculation. A common practice is mutual manipulation of the penis, another is oral intercourse, fellatio, which sometimes is reciprocated, sometimes not. Many homosexuals prefer penetration into the anus, which is potentially harmful to the partner. The anus is not designed to accommodate an erect penis and stretching the sphincter can cause pain and serious damage, such as rupture and hemorrhoids. This may result in fecal incontinence and carries the danger of infection for both parties.

Furthermore, it must be understood and accepted without question that anal intercourse is a very dangerous practice, for it is the most effective sexual means for spreading the AIDS virus. This applies to straights as well as gays, for some heterosexuals also engage in anal intercourse.

There is a wide range of behavior among homosexuals, depending on personality makeup. While the male and female roles are interchangeable, an individual usually assumes one role regularly. Some like to dress in women's clothing and makeup, which is referred to as "in drag," and are called "queens," but such a person may prefer to take the man's part in sexual relations, so external appearance is not necessarily an indication of the role played. Some queens prefer not to appear in public in drag, instead, they wear elaborate underthings to satisfy their needs. Male homosexuals who are reluctant to show their sexual preference are called "closet queens", or "in the closet", and those who make no secret of it are described as having "come out of the closet".

"Queens" are not to be confused with "transvestites", see page 114 of previous chapter.

Most homosexuals are promiscuous, and while two men may live together, their relationship is usually short lived. They change lovers frequently, even while sharing the same quarters, for loyalty is limited and sex is sought outside. This is not true of all gays, some of whom establish strong relationships that start out as sexual liaisons and evolve into solid friendships with no sexual activity. They may last a lifetime, however, they are uncommon.

Variety seems to be more important to homosexuals than to heterosexual men, although both may have the same impulse. Despite a good marriage, husbands often have fantasies about other women, but when a homosexual fantasizes, he usually takes action to find a new relationship. On the other hand, how many married men are monogamous? To our knowledge, there has never been a study to determine this, nor the monogamous incidence of women. It is common knowledge that "hanky-panky" is a way of life for some men and probably women, for it takes two to tango.

Some homosexuals hold that the admitted promiscuity of gays is due to the abuse, rejection and lack of respect to which they are subjected, and if this were removed and they had available the civil and legal rights of heterosexuals, this would be drastically reduced. The present trend, although slow, is in this direction.

There are many talented homosexuals who contribute more to society than the average heterosexual. Some are famous in the field of the dance, painting, music, writing and fashion design. They tend to have inborn aesthetic and artistic skills, which they are more apt to develop than straight individuals, who are principally occupied with family and making a living. Over the centuries, enormous contributions have been made by homosexuals such as Plato, Michelangelo and Oscar Wilde, the Irish dramatist who shocked English society during Victoria's reign.

The male homosexual is interested in new experiences. He is out for the pleasure of the moment and eager to try anything different. The more doing type leads a grasshopper life, has many partners and a variety of activities. If he has a satisfying orgasm, he doesn't worry about anything else. There are no lasting bonds and no concern for his partner. However, life is not easy for him for he has to develop a lifestyle that accommodates his sexual tendencies, and sooner or later collides with a social, psychological or physical problem to cope with, essentially alone.

So homosexuality presents hazards. As gays circulate from one encounter to the next, an infected man comes into contact with others and spreads disease. Thus, reservoirs of infection are established and are extremely difficult to eradicate. The tragedy is that while most conditions are amenable to treatment, the gay doesn't go for it soon enough and often arrives at the doctor's office too late. As a matter of fact, all men, gay and straight alike, have a tendency to ignore illness or the possibility of illness. Any doctor will admit that men don't pay attention to their health until they get really sick or have a bad pain or injury. They also tend to ignore preventive measures to remain healthy.

These diseases that are sexually transmitted by gays are bacterial and viral in nature. Some are precancerous and passed around so rapidly that they create a high percentage of incidence. This is not a health threat to the public except through the bisexual married man who goes into the city for a gay weekend and might take the infection back to his wife. A woman is more health conscious than most men and seeks medical attention more readily and sees that her husband does too.

Sexual activity involving the anus and rectum presents a health hazard that is becoming increasingly serious. Not only is there a rising incidence of the common infections which always plagued gay males, but AIDS (acquired immunity deficiency syndrome) was identified in 1981. This disease is insidious, as the depleted immune system is laid open to many disorders, including a rare cancer called Kaposi's sarcoma, and a previously unknown type of pneumonia, incurable so far.

It is true that the highest incidence of AIDS appeared to emanate from the gay male population when the HIV infection was first indentified. Once the method of its transfer from person to person was discovered, however, no segment of society has made greater strides than the gay male population. Since the 1970s, when gay men engaged in sex with almost every gay male they knew, matters have changed dramatically. The incidence of infection dropped fast and continues to drop, and is rising among heterosexuals and IV drug users and teenagers, most of whom are straight.

Gays function in different ways depending on personality. The extreme doer picks up a partner anywhere. He exchanges sexual advances in men's washrooms, on the street, or at "the baths," a favorite location for finding "tricks." The man he picks up is likely to be of the same type.

The more thinking homosexual doesn't participate in casual sex. He finds a partner through social channels and is apt to maintain the relationship longer. He is more conservative about admitting his sexual preference but is not ashamed of it. It is just not his temperament to flaunt it. He makes the rounds of social circles without being recognized as homosexual and engages in few frivolous sexual excesses, and the gay relationships he forms are healthy and caring. He has respect for his partners and treats them in a loving and affectionate manner.

A large group of men are bisexual, and have considerable experience with both men and women. Both influences are strong and a man is capable of falling in love with a woman or a man. His choice of a partner may be almost by chance and he may marry and have children. As he grows older, however, he cannot keep pace with the sexual demands of both wife and lover, and the weaker drive falters. He is apt to become disillusioned as the children grow into adolescence, family conflicts arise, and the implications of his lifestyle hit home. Furthermore, he may be having difficulty achieving an erection and orgasm with his wife which is apt to happen as he reaches middle age. As the sexual drive diminishes, he turns to the easiest stimulation, the homosexual, because that is what he basically responds to and enjoys most. Then he is likely to leave his wife for a calmer life with his lover. How does the wife feel? She is upset and feels at fault, reasoning that if she had been a better wife she could have kept him. Even though she blames herself, she feels cheated, and this makes her angry. The fault, if any, lies in marrying him knowing he was bisexual, and believing she could solidify their relationship by being a good and loving wife and having children. But how many women know you cannot change a bisexual into a heterosexual?

Sometimes these marriages last, but it is rare. If the wife is aware of her husband's leaning and is tolerant of it, she may want to keep the marriage together for the sake of the children, his business and social reasons. She has little sex life with her husband, however, and may have affairs or abstain from sex.

It is common belief that bisexuals marry to hide their sexual preference, but this is not true. It is usually because they fall in love. If they have children, they are very attached to them and make good fathers, and are often able to cope with them better than some wives. They may prefer to stay home and assume the mother's role, and frequently carry on a homosexual affair, sometimes surreptitiously, but often with the knowledge of their wives. As far as the children are concerned, most love their father and don't criticize him for his sexual activities. They are not angry or resentful, but very unhappy if he leaves the marriage.

It is not unusual for a bisexual man to have suicidal tendencies when he is young, because he is torn both ways and adjustment is difficult. Most make a comfortable decision, however, some have trouble accommodating to the dual role and seek psychiatric guidance. They don't look upon either choice as wrong but want to know whether there is an advantage in focusing on only one. As time goes on the dominant drive prevails, the homosexual.

In the gay community, the rate of suicide is one of the highest, however, this rate drops to the average level in areas where gays are allowed to participate in society on the same basis as the general population. Examples of such areas are New York, Chicago, San Francisco and certain European cities.

The word bisexual is misused by both professionals and the public, claiming that if a man or woman has one homosexual experience, he or she is bisexual. This is erroneous, for many heterosexuals admit to a homosexual encounter in early youth out of curiosity.

FEMALE HOMOSEXUALITY

Female homosexuals are usually referred to as lesbians, a term coined from the ancient Greek Island of Lesbos, where homosexual women were reputed to live. Lesbians are greatly outnumbered by male homosexuals, for reasons unknown, although the ratio between them has never been established. A guess would be two to one. It is known, however, from studies by the Kinsey Laboratory, that the origin of female homosexuality is the same as in males.

Formerly, male and female homosexuals did not associate on a regular basis. This has changed gradually in the last twenty years, although gay men don't visit bars frequented by lesbians, and lesbians don't visit gay male hangouts. They enjoy one another's company at parties and get togethers when both gay sexes are united, and in a gay parade or festival, where the mixing is free and easy. Furthermore, in many southwestern and southern cities there are bars in the gay districts, usually discos, that are known for the gay male and female clientele, and leaders of both groups join in an effort to eradicate any dichotomy that may exist. Moreover, gay men and women are getting to know one another more and more on a friendly personal basis and often become fast friends.

The most common sexual activity of lesbians is mutual masturbation to orgasm by manipulating the clitoris. Alternatively, the lesbian inserts one finger into the vagina and caresses the anus with another, while stroking the clitoris with a third. Partners may use the American position, woman on woman, and come to orgasm by rubbing the genitals together. The roles are interchangeable. Vibrators are used frequently and cunnilingus, stimulation of the clitoris with the tongue, is common. Dildoes are also popular. These are artificial penises made of rubber or plastic which can be strapped to the body to simulate a male penis.

While the male homosexual focuses on the penis, with erection and orgasm his goal, this is not the case with lesbians. Their sexual encounters are longer, and an important part involves kissing, hugging, and caressing one another, murmuring words of endearment. Their lovemaking reflects a woman's search for affection and love, as opposed to the largely physical sex act of the male. Lesbians tend to stay together for longer periods of time than many male gays, but the same pattern of jealousy, deception and conflict prevails.

There are bisexual women but the number is small and, as with men, the dominant drive takes precedence as time goes on. Marriages with men are scarce, but they do occur, and tend to last longer than those of male bisexuals. As they grow older, these women seem able to handle marriage, children and a lesbian relationship quite comfortably.

As homosexuals grow older, they are pitied for their lack of family and apparent loneliness, but a recent study by the National Institute of Mental Health reveals that homosexuals of both sexes feel quite comfortable about aging. While most don't have close family ties, they all have good friends and involvement in an interesting field, and many live with their lovers more compatibly than in their younger years.

WHAT IS AN AMBISEXUAL?

The term ambisexual was coined by Masters and Johnson to differentiate this group from the bisexual, and is applied to both males and females who are neither homosexual nor heterosexual. The incidence is not known, but the condition is significant enough to mention.

Kinsey's studies indicate that the heterosexual considers any form of bisexuality as corrupt homosexuality, and the homosexual thinks the ambisexual doesn't have the courage to commit him or herself to a homosexual lifestyle. The ambisexual, on the other hand, seldom if ever passes judgment on the sexual behavior of others. He and she appear to think, feel, and act from both hetero- and homosexual points of view and express no opinion about either. Both seem natural. In seeking a relationship, the sexual opportunity is the first consideration and the gender is secondary.

The ambisexual is not interested in a stable relationship or a family structure. It is not clear if this is due to the lack of capacity for love or another reason. By their own admission, ambisexuals lead lonely lives. Only time will reveal how they weather the process of aging.

DO HOMOSEXUALS INTERMARRY?

Occasionally, yes, but this is rare. However, the nurturing instinct can be strong in both sexes and foster the desire for children, which is the motivating factor. In the marriage, the parenting is shared, but sexual activity is with those of their own sex.

Interesting enough, there are a few instances of an unusual phenomenon, a "menage à trois", whereby two men and a woman live together for the purpose of bringing children into the world, which illustrates the strong drive to have children, although all three are homosexual. One threesome pooled their resources, bought a house and moved in together. Soon, a little girl was born to the woman, and was loved and nurtured by all three. No one knew which of the two men was the father. They did not want to know. The four lived as a family, the mother continuing her lesbian relationships and the men their homosexual affiliations. Presumably, the child grew up normally in a loving family.

GAY ACTIVISM

Before the 1960s and 1970s, both male and female homosexuals had no forum from which to exert political pressure on the heterosexual world, which had oppressed them, ridiculed them, and denied them their constitutional rights of free speech, assembly and other civil liberties. The only place they could congregate was in the gay bars, where they were able to speak freely with one another about gay political issues. There were no rallies for the gay community and no political groups or lobbies.

In the bars, drag had its place and gradually drag shows began to appear, capturing the group's attention and building a sense of identity and belonging. Here, gays could share their frustrations and air the constant rejections that they were subjected to daily. So, over the years, they developed into a strong entity, dedicated to ameliorating the negative attitudes they faced every day. They yearned to be accepted as individuals and respected for what they were and not reviled for their sexual orientation.

Thus, the concept of "drag" as a political tool began in the gay bars and finally emerged into the open and the streets, resulting in rallies, parades and so forth. These activities helped to eradicate the feeling of isolation and of being different, a concept that had been thrust upon them and which they had always had to live with. By the 1990s, gays had gained access to more traditional segments of the power structure and established their own churches and clubs and organizations.

The next step forward is gays' civil rights. Conditions have improved somewhat, as a few states have passed anti-discrimination laws and the recognition of the rights of individuals, but nowhere do gay couples, male or female, enjoy the privileges that the rest of us take for granted. The religious and civil ceremonies of marriage cannot be performed on gay couples, and the courts don't recognize their relationship in legal matters. For example, gays have no protection in housing, jobs, health insurance or even the military, from which they are discharged if their sexual orientation is discovered.

It is under such a burden that all gay persons live.

8

THE MEANING OF PSYCHOSO-MATIC MEDICINE

Psychosomatic medicine is not new. It was first described in ancient Chinese medical literature, and again in 500 B.C. by Hippocrates, who claimed that doctors should know the "whole of things" in order to effect cures. Through the ages, this was reiterated by Socrates and the Roman physicians Soranus and Aurelianus, who practiced psychotherapy to relieve their patients' physical illnesses. The same philosophies prevailed in the Middle Ages, and it was well known early in the nineteenth century that strong emotional upheavals could result in disease, grief could cause illness, and one could, in fact, die of a "broken heart".

What happened to the whole person? There is a valid answer. Later in the nineteenth century Pasteur's work caused such excitement that doctors came to believe that there must be a special bacterium or organism responsible for every disease. Thus, physicians were trained to treat the disease and not the person. The concept of the while person was shoved to the back burner, where it remained until recently. Today, the holistic approach to medicine is based on the treatment of the whole person, physically, mentally, and spiritually.

What does psychosomatic mean? The word comes from the Greek "psyche," mind, and "soma," body, or mind/body. It was coined by physicians in the 1940s, when they became aware that emotions and personality as well as physical factors can increase the intensity of an illness and influence its onset, length and severity.

Somatopsychic, the reverse of psychosomatic, or body/mind, can also be used in describing an illness, for an illness that attacks the body also affects the mind. For example, acne, which is caused by an over supply of oil secreted by skin pores, creates an emotional reaction. The person is ashamed of his appearance, and the pores secrete more oil, worsening the acne.

What is a psychosomatic illness? It is when the nervous system influences the body in such a way that an illness follows. However, first it is essential that a thorough physical work-up be done to rule out physical disease. This will make sure that the mind is responsible. Every system in the body, such as eating, eliminating, coughing, urinating, heart rate, and intestinal activity, can be influenced positively or adversely by the nervous system. These systems can also be affected by infection, an organism, an accident or the malfunction of an organ.

Psychosomatic medicine is divided into many areas and doctors vary in their understanding and application of the term. Many studies have been made but there is no consensus as to the cause, treatment or classification of these conditions, because the interrelationship between mind and body is poorly understood. Some consider psychosomatic medicine a specialty, and there are doctors who are experts in the field, but the scope is so broad and its delineation so blurred that the word is no longer adequate.

Should the term be discarded? No, we are saddled with it because it is used universally, but it is unfortunate that its true meaning has been distorted. Doctors and laymen alike interpret it one way, that the mind is doing something to the body to make it sick. Some doctors use the word, "functional" for psychosomatic, which further confuses the patient. When explained, however, some people become infuriated and others upset, and construe the diagnosis as mental illness, or worse, insanity. It is unfortunate that many people are still ashamed of mental illness and do not know that, in medical parlance, there is no such word as insanity.

So it is finally accepted that there are ties between the mind and the body that cause them to react upon one another. But how do they react? The mind can influence the body to bring about or prevent disease, and the body, in illness, can manipulate the mind into a state of anxiety. We have also discovered that the mind can control functions of the autonomic nervous system, like the heartbeat, digestion and the circulation. These had previously been considered solely under the command of a section of the brain called the hypothalamus. Thus, the mind and the body are as one. A simple way to understand this is to visualize a human being as a set of scales, one side the body, the other the mind. Most of the time they balance. This is called "homeostasis." When one outweighs the other, illness occurs. If the body doesn't supply enough sugar to the brain, or if the brain doesn't supply the appropriate nervous impulses to the body, there is malfunction. The implication is that every system should be performing at its best all the time. Of course, this doesn't happen, but a slight dip of the scale one way or the other can occur and be easily put back in balance by a minor adjustment. How do we do this?

Our body systems check themselves, and compensate for an imbalance. If the kidneys work too fast, we go to the bathroom more often, if the nervous system is overactive, the body calls for more food or rest. When we don't pay attention, we might get sick. But unless the mind/body interchange is severely off, we adjust to imbalances. So it is a good idea for the mind to listen to its body.

We don't expect the automobile to run indefinitely without changing the oil, replacing the filters and spark plugs or having the brakes relined. We feed it with gas just as we feed our bodies. Both use substances that cause wear and tear. The body, like a car, sometimes needs help in repairing itself. Our teeth need filling, diabetics replace the insulin they can no longer produce, and we take calcium for strong bones as we grow older. These are not psychosomatic conditions, but normal wear and tear.

But if something breaks down, we hit the ceiling. "I am never sick! What is happening? Am I falling apart?" Of course not, we just need a little repairing. If we do become ill, an emotional reaction muddies the waters. This is the somatopsychic influence, the influence of the body on the mind. We get the flu and are upset about missing work. And we are angry and feel guilty for being ill. Our emotions are working overtime, and emotional stress can bring on illness, the antithesis of the above. So it doesn't matter which comes first, the emotions or the illness, each works on the other. The loss of a loved one, the sudden death of a dear friend, or the break-up of a romance can disturb the body's homeostasis, thereby lowering the immune system, making it vulnerable to infection or disease, and the person comes down with a cold. Even a minor event can produce lowered immunity in some people. As we look back on life, we all have had this experience.

Listen to your body. It knows what it is doing even when you and the doctor may not. When you have an infection, you develop a fever and your white cells increase to fight it. This is the body's natural response. Given rest and time, the fever will come down. You may rush in to treat it, and end up fighting off these responses. If you are concerned, lie in a hot bath for fifteen minutes and the heat will fight the infection. Given a chance, your body will heal itself.

Here is an example of an emotionally induced condition. Marian's baby was a few months old when her daughter-in-law brought her first born home. Marian was teaching the young mother how to care for the baby, when she developed diarrhea and was afraid she might give it to the baby. Her physician found nothing wrong, and diagnosed a psychosomatic reaction to a difficult situation. Marian's son married while in college against his parents' wishes, and the arrival of the baby compounded the shock. Although reluctantly, she helped her daughter-in-law, for if she had not, she would have felt guilty. In that event, her condition may have become worse.

An emotional blast can turn inward or outward. We can take out our frustrations on family or become depressed. We could loose appetite, have diarrhea or a rapid heartbeat and hyperventilate. Or we could have none of these reactions. What began as anger at a minor illness developed into a chain of emotional and physical symptoms feeding into one another. And the doctor has to understand the whole history before he can make a correct diagnosis. He can't come into the middle of the picture, pick out a symptom and treat it successfully. So we have to cooperate with him and tell him everything.

We repeat, the correct diagnosis is important and must be made before starting treatment. The real challenge in psychosomatic medicine is in deciding how much of the illness comes from the mind and how much from the body. This requires a team approach by the internist and the psychiatrist, and the first step is to know the patient as a whole human being. This method has been used for a relatively short time and has proved to be successful. The doctors, however, have difficulty working together because they speak different languages, the internist and the psychiatrist.

To make a diagnosis is difficult, and often the decision is psychosomatic. Mistakes are made by an inadequate work-up and jumping to conclusions. When a doctor can't make a diagnosis, he tells the patient: "It's your nerves," or "It's emotional," or "There's nothing wrong, it is in your head." And how does the patient feel? "I must be sick in the head." The cycle of mind/body-body/mind speeds up and the condition worsens. We see this with diseases of the skin, allergies, asthma, stomachache, diarrhea, loss of appetite, excessive appetite, ulcers, and serious conditions like ulcerative colitis.

This is an example of misdiagnosis. Christopher is depressed to the point of wanting to take his life because of prolonged diarrhea, loss of appetite and weight loss. Several specialists found nothing wrong, and psychiatrists treated his depression without success. After many drugs and therapies, he saw a doctor who ran more tests and found a parasitic infection which was promptly treated and cured. This illustrates the result of inadequate diagnosis. The patient's condition so depleted him that he could not live a normal life, and depression resulted. This demonstrates the effect of mind on body and vice versa, with mental and physical conditions worsening to an almost fatal conclusion.

So the doctor looks at both the body and the mind and determines how they are interacting. He gets to know his patient well, his personality and emotional makeup, and does a thorough physical work-up. In making the diagnosis, psychosomatic illness should be considered only after all physical causes have been ruled out.

Does everybody get psychosomatic illnesses? Everybody can, but not everyone does. The susceptibility is not tied to thinking and doing, but involved with personality, emotional state, and life situation. It's like the chicken or the egg syndrome. Did something upset you, or did you come down with the flu first?

How can we keep this from happening to us? Accept your health, good or bad, with a positive attitude. Deal with yourself as you are, understand your body and know that at times it is not going to work right. Don't deny it if it doesn't, and it is equally important not to think you might have an illness. Set the goal of being as well as you can be. Believe that if you do develop an illness, you will get better. Accept it and deal with it positively. Don't fall victim to it. Sometimes you don't need help, sometimes you need a home remedy, sometimes you need a doctor.

Women are better at this than men. They have menstrual periods and bear babies. Men push being ill aside and deny they are sick, believing they will die if they admit it. It's foolish to expect to be in top shape all the time. We can lose an arm or a leg and be a healthy person. We can have cancer and be a healthy person, or a heart condition or diabetes. It's all in the attitude, and attitude can help avoid the emotional reaction that makes an illness last longer. Serious conditions can also be handled this way, by giving the body free rein to do its healing without interference from the psyche. This frame of mind can be cultivated, but it isn't easy.

How are psychosomatic/somatopsychic illnesses treated? Most are self-limiting and go away as quickly as they came, and if superimposed upon a physical illness, the treatment of that will eliminate the other. However, it the condition persists, psychotherapy is successful in every case.

How did the human race exist for four million years without doctors? Because the body is built to heal itself. Does the doctor mend a broken leg or cure a cold? No, we do. Most psychosomatic illnesses go away by themselves, which means they are self-limiting, like most illnesses. We don't know how, but we know that it happens.

9

NEUROTIC TENDENCIES ARE NATURAL DEFENSES

Everyone has nervous reactions to certain situations. We call these reactions neurotic tendencies. Everyone has them, some people have more, some less, depending on personality makeup. It is nothing to be ashamed of. The term neurotic tendency may be misleading. They are not neuroses. however, if a neurosis does occur, it is readily treatable. Neurotic tendencies are the uncomfortable feelings we experience such as anxiety, insecurity and depression. In this chapter we will discuss the most common.

Anxiety is a feeling of tension, apprehension, indecisiveness, foreboding, rolled into one. It is a natural reaction to challenge. It is relatively constant, but flares up as we face a challenge, whether minor or major, such as a flat tire, the angry word of a friend, a fire in the broiler, an accident, the first day on a new job. Watching our children board the school bus can create anxiety, so can catching a train or plane. In fact, anxiety is essential for meeting life's obstacles, and is a major component of drive.

Is it a common condition? Yes, anxiety is universal, and we can learn to deal with it and put it to work for us. Properly used, it enhances life, but loses its usefulness when disregarded or masked by alcohol, tranquilizers or other drugs. One facet of anxiety is apprehension, which is linked to the healthy side of paranoia and keeps us out of danger. It gets the adrenalin flowing and helps us do a better job. Studies show that apprehension before a stressful situation results in a superior performance, keying up mind and body for a special effort.

Competition is a source of anxiety. Society sets goals for us all, so competition intrudes on every phase of life: social, personal, recreational, financial, sexual. Top performance is so entrenched in our culture that self-esteem is directly related to success, and constant striving toward objectives beyond our capability produces anxiety. Is anxiety the same as stress? No, but each causes the other, stress from without and anxiety from within. Both are important to the fulfillment of goals.

Normal anxiety can become severe following a devastating life event such as an accident or a death in the family, but if it becomes chronic and continues without letup, interfering with normal activity, professional help is advisable.

Insecurity is a common tendency. and its development depends on the lack of fulfillment in childhood of three basic needs, love, approval, and consistency. Parents are especially important, for their love is as vital as food and shelter to the development of a child's personality. Parental acceptance of children as they are, and consistency of love and approval helps them emerge as secure adults, ensuring emotional security.Research proved this point years ago when babies in institutions were left alone except for regular feedings.

They were not picked up when they cried or fondled or played with. In the absence of affection and physical contact, many lost their appetites and died for no reason that could be determined. Subsequent studies showed that babies who got tender, loving care flourished and grew into happy, healthy children. This led to the development of surrogate mother programs for orphaned and abandoned little ones.

We all feel insecure at times. It is an unpleasant, uncomfortable emotion. The best remedy is the love, approval and understanding of someone close. Attention and admiration from other sources boost the ego, and help us meet the demands of our jobs and social obligations. However, this must be genuine, not superficial flattery. Insecurity can get out of hand if faced with severe emotional stress, and may provoke a person to turn to escapism, such as alcohol or drugs. Some over compensate and join a religious cult or bury themselves in work or recreation to the neglect of family and friends. Whatever is done, is done in extreme with a frantic drive to find security.

Everyone has experienced *depression* to one degree or another, which is a subtle change in awareness of how we feel. We are all subject to swings of mood up and down for no apparent reason, and all mood changes are related to both internal and external pressures. Some people travel on an even keel, some have minor ups and downs, while others experience deep valleys of depression, but the most common pattern is episodes of depression without elation. The seasons of the year have an effect on mood. Also, mood can plummet under adversity, accident, surgery and an unhappy life event. But contrary to what we may think, studies reveal no relationship to barometric pressure, the phases of the moon, tide fluctuations, the positions of the stars or other phenomena of nature.

Mood swings may be temporary and the extreme moods, either up or down, can vanish naturally without treatment. Abnormally high or low moods are caused by fluctuations of the chemical balance in brain cells. We all experience them, and knowing we all share them alleviates the feeling of aloneness, and we can survive without shame or damage.

There are two kinds of depression. Reactive depression, the most common, and chemical depression. Reactive depression may result from an emotional shock, such as the death of a loved one, a job loss, a broken love affair or a financial setback. A physical shock, such as an accident, a serious illness, or an incurable disease can also trigger depression, and repressed anger may find its outlet this way. The response to these pressures is individual, what depresses one person may not depress another or to the same degree.

There is also reactive elation. Since mood moves both up and down, certain events can send it very high. Extreme elation is just as disturbing to emotional balance as deep depression, for it can cause compulsive behavior that produces guilt and subsequent depression. For example, Roger wins a million dollars in the sweepstakes. He is euphoric. He buys a Rolls Royce, sells his house, buys another and spends a fortune on furnishings. He entertains his family and friends and gives them expensive presents. Soon the money is gone and he sinks into depression. People can react this way.

Reaction to a life crisis can result in complaints other than depression. These may be headaches, fatigue, vague pains, nausea, constipation, heartburn and irritability. Thus, the psyche is trying to ward off depression by substituting physical symptoms. Other reactions may be weight gain due to compulsive eating, drinking more, smoking marijuana, taking tranquilizers or hard drugs in an effort to escape. This may serve temporarily as an anesthetic but there is still a risk of falling into depression, especially if alcohol is resorted to, because alcohol is a mental as well as a physical depressant.

The symptoms of reactive and chemical depression are similar, and it is difficult for any but a skilled physician to tell them apart. This is important because the treatment differs, reactive depression by psychotherapy, chemical depression by anti-depressant medication. Reactive depression comes and goes, chemical depression is deeper and much more persistent. Reactive depression appears after a distressing episode in life and can cause great mental and sometimes physical suffering. The old adage says "time heals all wounds" and this holds true for reactive depression.

Around 500 B.C. at the Delphic Oracle, someone inscribed in Greek the words "Know thyself." We believe this is a first step in helping alleviate depression. Also, learn what affects your mood, and try to bring the high and low moods closer together by easing the pressures around you. You can do this by knowing your personality and your emotional, intellectual and physical capacities for work, family and social life. The thinker suffers more from anxiety than the doer, and high energy can drive you beyond your capability. So realistic goal setting is important as well as the maintenance of physical well-being.

If you haven't recovered after a reasonable period of time, psychotherapy can help. Tell the doctor the recent events in your life and your physical and mental symptoms. A good rapport, with open communication, is essential in order to benefit from therapy.

Next, listen to your doctor with an open mind. He may not make specific recommendations but will interpret your thinking and soon you will be discussing means of coming closer to your goals. And what are your goals? Do you need a career change? Should you move to another part of the country? He will allow you to make your own decisions and with his objective viewpoint you can examine the ideas you have with him as a credible listener and he will guide you to a better insight so you can come to rational conclusions. Although you feel you will never be well again, you will soon find your deeper, true self and before you know it, you have worked your problems out and come to sensible decisions.

During this time, it is important to maintain physical health. Good nutrition, exercise and adequate sleep are essential and curative. You may need tranquilizers to begin with, but psychotherapy without medication is usually more effective, and your well-being will become established without this support. Though you feel you will never be yourself again, the doctor will assure you that you will, and that his wide experience with similar cases allows him to predict accurately.

HYPOCHONDRIA

Hypochondria is a fairly prevalent disease. Some experts suggest that half of all doctor visits are instigated by hypochondria. In fact, it may be that all of us are susceptible to some extent at a time during our lives. This is evident in the phenomenon called "medical student's disease" which three-quarters of medical students experience during the course of their schooling. They develop symptoms of the disease they are studying which disappear as they move on to another subject.

Psychiatrists, who have studied hypochondria extensively, maintain that hypochondriacs are more receptive to pain and more in tune with their body functions than others, and appear to have a heightened awareness of their bodies. They constantly complain of "funny feelings", minor aches and pains and twinges which most people have, but ignore. However, as hypochondriacs have this extreme and acute sensitivity, it is understandable that the smallest pain is accentuated and can become magnified to the point of a real concern that a serious disease is pending.

Hypochondria is common to both men and women, and is classified into two groups. Those who make up the largest are really afraid a serious condition is causing their symptoms and that their doctors are going to find a fatal disease. The hypochondriac is always complaining of physical problems. He is absorbed in them and talks endlessly about them. His sensitivity causes an exaggerated sense of distress. While his symptoms are usually non-existent or greatly magnified the hypochondriac's pains are very real indeed. Despite his complaints, however, he functions well in his work and in other aspects of life.

A smaller group are persons with a strong paranoid trend who use illness to evade responsibility. They learn early in life how to manipulate others by their moanings and groanings in order to avoid doing things they dislike. They use their pains and aches as an excuse not to work very hard, with the added bonus that people feel sorry for them and give them the attention they crave. This kind of maneuvering becomes a way of life, and some get away with it and manage to make a living, taking all the help and consideration they can. Others lose the respect of their friends and wear out the patience of their families.

The hypochondriac usually develops symptoms by early adulthood. Most have transient aches and pains during childhood described as "growing pains." They may be chronically tired, lethargic, irritable, and talkative. Sleep is disturbed by nightmares. While these signs are intermittent during childhood, a pattern becomes established by the time they are grown up. The symptoms can be confusing and there is no set pattern. Every patient's complaints differ, and no two doctors agree on what they have been told. It may be weakness and fatigue, or vague aches and pains moving from place to place. There are gastrointestinal symptoms, irritability, insomnia, and chronic physical exhaustion. The condition is poorly understood, the underlying cause unknown. It is clear, however, that life situations combined with certain personality traits are partly responsible, and it could be that a traumatic experience, a depression or a feeling of inadequacy could set it off.

Another explanation may be the underproduction of endorphins in the brain, which is the chemical that provides anesthesia for pain, making some people overreact to the minor pains we all have. We just don't know. There is usually nothing physically wrong, but the hypochondriac's paranoid tendency never allows him to accept this, so he seeks relief from one doctor after another. In essence, his complaints come from his mind, making it difficult to diagnose and treat them.

Right at this moment assess our own bodies. We probably have a mild discomfort, an itch, a stubbed toe hurts, the back aches from sitting. But we don't dwell on these aggravations, we brush them aside, never thinking we may end up with a major disease. The hypochondriac's pain, however, doesn't brush away. It seems major and bothers him constantly and he is afraid it is serious.

Men pay less attention than women to signs of something wrong with their bodies. They want to enjoy life and keep active, and are unwilling to admit to disability. It is the nature of women, however, to be aware of what is happening to their bodies and they seek medical advice far more promptly than men. There is a middle ground, however, between hypochondria and burying your head in the sand.

After a day's work, a change of pace is reviving and we enjoy the evening. Not so the hypochondriac. He feels tired when he gets up in the morning, tired all day and an evening of fun does not revive him. He is too tired and sick to go anywhere or do anything for pleasure, or to indulge in sports or exercise. He bemoans the fact that he can't, yet seems to revel in his helplessness. A trace of this is a common human trait, which we all have at times.

Some hypochondriacs have low self-esteem, and hold on to their symptoms, which gives them a sense of identity, boosting their egos. They use symptoms as a crutch to prove they are somebody. Attention relieves their guilt, but this only perpetuates the condition, which they deny is psychosomatic. They consider that demeaning and only a physical disease is acceptable. It also is an excuse to duck responsibilities.

The hypochondriac visits one doctor after another looking for the answer he wants to hear—that he has a disease. If he admits how many doctors he has seen, the picture would be clearer, but no physician will make a diagnosis on such evidence. So the round of tests begins again to make sure there is no organic cause. This focuses attention on the patient, which is what he is after. Sometimes he says he is feeling better, only to report the next day that he is worse. Moreover, he takes pleasure in making it hard for the doctor by cancelling tests, refusing to take medication and being generally uncooperative. This is frustrating to the doctor who is often blamed for adding to his suffering.

It is difficult to diagnose hypochondria. The symptoms are vague, and if the patient has been making the rounds of physicians' offices, it is easy to assume that he is a hypochondriac. However a physical condition can account for the complaints, therefore a thorough work-up followed by a psychiatric examination is in order. The patient is delighted if the doctor turns up a reason for his symptoms. It may be an ulcer or gallstones or high blood pressure, but now he has something to blame and would cheerfully undergo surgery, in fact might even demand it. If the final diagnosis is hypochondria and the doctor explains that the symptoms are imaginary, the patient becomes angry and sets out to find another doctor.

How is hypochondria treated? There is no specific method. Each patient is evaluated on the basis of personality, history and life situation. Psychotherapy is successful in many cases, and drugs in selected cases. The doctor may recommend changes in lifestyle, job, personal relationships, and so forth. If the patient is agreeable, there is a good chance his symptoms will improve. If he is not, they are slim.

Hypochondriacs are victims of their personalities. They have low energy, average intelligence and are inclined to be the doing type. They come from all walks of life and all types of occupations. They have difficulty dealing with life's problems and are unable to accept others whose personalities differ from theirs. Most function fairly well. An example is "Old Bones," an outstanding ball player. He comes to the ball park announcing that he feels terribly, then proves to be the best player. He complains but always outperforms the others. This is typical of the hypochondriac without a paranoid tendency, with a paranoid tendency, he would use his symptoms to get pity and avoid playing.

Studies show that intelligence influences the type of complaints in hypochondria. Educated people show a lower incidence and are more responsive to treatment. Patients reject the possibility that personal problems cause their illness, and expect the doctor to cure them without cooperation on their part. More intelligent patients can usually be helped once they accept the fact that a physical condition is not responsible.

Another fairly common neurotic tendency is *hysterics*. which is not to be confused with *hysteria*. A woman, weeping uncontrollably, screaming and throwing herself about is having hysterics. It is an over emotional reaction to stress or frustration. Some women go into hysterics pretending to hurt themselves. They seldom do, but like to give that impression. Temper tantrums in children are hysterics, and a child holding his breath until blue in the face. It is a form of manipulation and a call for attention or to force someone into doing one's will. These are all elements of paranoia. Men are less prone than women to have hysterics, as they are inclined to keep their emotions inside. Instead, they become withdrawn, sullen and hostile, or non-communicative.

What is hysteria? Hysteria is rare in men and affects women of the doing type who don't think things out. It is a primitive response, and those who are prone react primitively in other ways as well. It doesn't come from a single cause and the symptoms so closely resemble disease that a correct diagnosis is difficult.

Hysteria is a product of the mind, causing the body to convert emotion into physical signs. For example, there are women who experience false pregnancies, with enlargement of the abdomen and cessation of menstrual periods. Tests prove the condition to be hysteria, triggered by an intense desire to have children and the failure to conceive.

Sudden paralysis is not uncommon in hysteria. Invariably, the symptoms show up in the part of the body related to the cause. For example, Helen suddenly developed paralysis of the legs and pelvis. She had not been injured and physical examination revealed no cause, so a diagnosis of hysteria was made. Psychotherapy revealed a broken love affair. The paralysis was in the site of her frustration, the sex organs.

Patricia slapped her boy friend in the face. He left her in a huff. Immediately, her hand became paralyzed from the wrist down. Frightened, she went to the emergency room and was hospitalized for tests. When no physical cause was found, she was referred to a psychiatrist who treated her by psychotherapy. Within two days, the paralysis disappeared.

Hysteria is the great imitator. It takes many forms and resembles symptoms of many diseases. A woman may suddenly become blind or go into convulsions, which puzzles the physician, but he can make a diagnosis only after a thorough examination. Another form is amnesia. A woman leaves the house and becomes disoriented. Soon, she finds herself in a strange location with no knowledge of how she got there, and doesn't remember her name or where she lives.

What sort of woman has hysteria? She tends to be emotionally unstable and, in many cases, gives the impression of seductiveness, which may or may not be intentional. She is inclined to be self-centered, and sometimes overreacts to get attention, which is her overpowering need. She can be very attractive in a social group but is usually extremely insecure, which leads to severe anxiety.

An hysterical patient is unconcerned about what seems to be a serious illness. She may become blind, deaf, or partially paralyzed and show no fear. As she claims to be severely ill, this is an indication of hysteria and a clue for the physician. A common mistake is to suspect physical disease, and a physical examination should always be performed to make certain no disease is present.

Hysteria used to be fashionable. Historical novels show instances of hysterical paralysis in women, which disappears when their wishes are granted. In olden days, it was considered romantic for a lady to faint in her lover's arms. Someone ran for the smelling salts and a whiff quickly aroused the fainting beauty.

Hysteria is contagious. These are common examples. We see a crowd and hurry to find out what is going on. Is there a fight? Is someone hurt? We have to know. At the scene of an accident, people gather around watching, but only a few help. Stand alone at a counter in a department store staring at something in the showcase, and soon you will be joined by one or two people. Often we are held up on the highway, and when the log jam breaks, the delay turns out to be rubber necking at an accident in the opposite lane. This shows the contagious element of hysteria. We follow one another like lemmings.

A more serious manifestation is mass hysteria. When people gather together under conditions that can be stressful, there is the chance of an outbreak. A person becomes ill and soon others complain of the same. Complaints may be fainting, headache, difficulty in breathing, nausea and vomiting. Doctors are called in. If examinations and tests eliminate medical causes, the diagnosis is mass hysteria. This phenomenon is sparked by a neurotic tendency. What happens is that emotions brought about by the environment stimulate the body to produce symptoms, and these are accentuated by paranoid fear of the unknown. What kind of stress causes mass hysteria? Concern today about toxic wastes provides fertile ground for an outbreak. It has occurred in towns that were sprayed with insecticides. People complained of dizziness, headache and general malaise, with symptoms ranging from mild to severe and incapacitating. When disease was ruled out, complaints disappeared as fast as they came.

Recently, a newspaper ran this story. A plant was shut down because an employee felt sick and blamed the air. Another succumbed. and another until most of the workers were ill and the plant had to close for the day. The air was tested and was not bad. This was mass hysteria, and the emotion behind it is fear. Is this going to happen to me is the question in everyone's mind.

Who succumbs to mass hysteria? We don't know which personality types are vulnerable. Usually, up to forty percent of a group is afflicted, more women than men in a ratio of about sixty to forty, and young people, especially girls. Sixty percent of recorded events occurred in schools, often coinciding with stress associated with examinations, sports competition or performances.

Mass hysteria is suspected if the victims are normally healthy, if there are signs such as fainting and hyperventilation, if the illness spreads quickly and clears up as rapidly as it appeared. Another sign is if it reappears when the same individuals return to the site where it first occurred.

Psychotherapy and hypnosis are the treatments for hysteria, separately or together. Drugs and tranquilizers do no good. Prognosis is excellent.

A characteristic of personality which we all carry is called *obsessive behavior*. These are examples. Do you count the steps as you walk upstairs? Do you avoid stepping on the cracks in the sidewalks? Do you count the cars passing by as you wait to cross the street? Do you notice how a man keeps arranging the articles on his desk as he talks to you? Do you know a woman who wipes off the kitchen counters over and over? These are manifestations of obsessive behavior everyone has to some degree and in one form or another. They are little tricks we develop which become part of us and of which we are mostly unaware. They are harmless and are the idiosyncrasies that express our uniqueness.

If we are the thinking type, we show more of this behavior due to concern about details and an inclination for formalities. We spend minutes getting organized and arranging the papers on the desk before settling down to work, to the neglect of more important things. When we are finally ready, we focus on the minor jobs and delay the major.

Occasionally, obsessiveness builds up until it begins to interfere with daily routine. We spend so much time satisfying these needs that we neglect our obligations, even though common sense tells us to stop. At this point such behavior is no longer normal and help is needed. Psychotherapy offers a favorable outcome in mild cases. Severe obsessive disorder is a serious and disabling illness that requires expert treatment and modern medication.

PANIC ATTACKS

What is a panic attack? It is the sudden onset of a disabling fear. The dictionary states this condition is "a sudden, overwhelming fear, with or without cause that produces hysterical or irrational behavior." It is not a neurosis, but can become one when it happens often and interferes with a person's life. There are many manifestations of a panic attack. No one has every symptom at one time but additional symptoms may develop if the condition is not treated. They appear without obvious provocation and terror sets in. The person feels unable to breathe, is faint and dizzy, the heart beats rapidly. There may be trembling, shaking, and pains in the chest, suggesting a heart attack, the thought of which exacerbates the symptoms.

It is estimated that twenty-four million Americans experience panic associated with intense anxiety at some time in their lives, more women than men. Attacks may occur only once or several times or often. An attack can happen two or three times a day or only every month or two. Some are afflicted only when under stress, others when there is no stress. There is no general pattern, but disabling fear is similar in each case. Because so many suffer from this condition, we are covering it in detail.

Hyperventilation may be the first symptom of an attack, then panic and overriding fear. For example, a woman was on a train when suddenly she experienced a frightening feeling that she could not get enough air, so she breathed faster and faster and felt dizzy and weak. She didn't know what was happening to her for she had always been healthy. She got off the train at the next stop, shaking, her legs like butter. She struggled to a taxi and begged to be taken to a doctor's office. The doctor gave her a sedative and she promptly recovered, but it was a harrowing experience.

Her problem was hyperventilation due to the stressful mission she was on. Our bodies require a balance of oxygen and carbon dioxide taken into the lungs with each breath. Extreme stress or fear touches off a mechanism whereby we breath faster and faster, thereby taking in large amounts of oxygen and blowing out carbon dioxide. This causes an imbalance in the blood which brings on the symptoms of rapid heart beat, weak arms and legs, dizziness, lightheadedness, ringing in the ears and a sense of air hunger. The struggle to breathe more deeply and more rapidly increases the imbalance and causes panic. We know that oxygen is essential to life, and carbon dioxide is a poison. Too much oxygen, however, can be poisonous too. We need both gases in the proper amounts.

What to do? To correct this imbalance, keep the mouth shut, close one nostril with a forefinger and breathe gently through the other. In ten seconds symptoms will disappear. It is amazing how quickly the body adjusts to normal if allowed to do its thing. Exercise also uses up the excess oxygen, so a vigorous run will do the trick as well.

Hyperventilation can be produced and as easily reversed. Sit still and take in seven to ten deep breaths. Almost immediately there will be air hunger with dizziness and weakness. Some people have a delicate oxygen/carbon dioxide balance and respond more rapidly than others, but this is an example of how closely body and mind are linked. The physical distress produces the emotional reactions which in turn, trigger the physical response that can either cure or aggravate the condition. If the panicky feeling causes deeper breathing, the adrenalin output increases, setting off the "fight or flight" mechanism. And panic is a primitive response that makes clear and rational thinking impossible.

Panic attacks can be triggered by emotion, but often they become a pattern which repeats itself daily, and this is destructive to daily living. They are linked to depression and treating the depression sometimes cures the attacks. They are often coupled with the use of tranquilizers taken to relieve anxiety, which helps the anxiety but doesn't cure it. Alcohol can also touch off a panic attack, but the basic cause is the lack of physical activity. Many patients are cured by cutting out the drugs and exercising.

Two-thirds of sufferers of panic attacks develop a phobia about the place an attack can occur. There are two types, closed in places (claustrophobia) and open spaces (agoraphobia). It can happen in elevators, churches, crowds, airplanes, corridors, cars or stores. Terror strikes rapidly with a choking sensation, a smothered feeling, pain in the chest, or dizziness, numbness or tingling of the hands or feet, faintness and trembling, or a combination of these. The reaction is "Please, get me out of here!" The fear of open spaces can occur in the supermarket, taking a walk, climbing a mountain, looking out of an airplane, crossing a bridge, anywhere in the open.

A person never knows when panic can happen or what triggers it, but those who are prone learn to be prepared by avoiding situations such as sitting in the middle seat of the airplane, going to the theatre, or locking the door of the bathroom. It is of the utmost importance to be sure of a quick and easy exit.

Victims of panic attacks suffer longer than the attack lasts, which is merely minutes, but the effects can be prolonged and color a person's life. Anything as frightening as a panic attack usually send you to medical care, and you may take the symptoms literally, convinced you are dying, losing your mind, being choked or having a heart attack. Fortunately, the panic soon subsides, but a few sufferers become confined to home, only venturing out with someone they can trust. More common is that the anticipation of an attack may prevent a person from going to the location or taking the trip where an attack occurred. This can keep a business man off planes, out of taxis, restaurants and hotels, restricting his career. Some persons avoid sexual relations because of the anticipation of an attack. One woman refrained from sexual interplay due to fear of being smothered, thus inducing hyperventilation.

There are other manifestations of the side effects of panic attacks. Some patients suffer from insomnia, others abuse alcohol and drugs, caffeine is toxic to some, and can trigger an attack. Another is depression brought on by the patient's inability to lead a normal life.

The diagnosis of panic disorder can readily be missed. First, is the need for a thorough physical examination, as many cases are associated with abnormal heart rhythms or defective valve function. These are easily treated, resulting in the termination of attacks. Chemical depression, drugs or alcohol abuse are frequent causes, and hyperventilation alone can be the culprit. Studies show that panic attacks tend to run in families, so heredity may be involved. Aside from these possibilities, other causes are less well understood. Once a cause is determined, however, most cases can be enormously benefited by the proper therapy, and although each case is different, almost all can be treated successfully.

PHOBIAS

What is a phobia? The word comes from the Greek phobos, meaning fear, and everybody has some tendency to them. There are two kinds, those associated with things, such as germs, animals, flying objects, insects, and those pertaining to surroundings, such as heights, lightning, the dark, stage fright, flying, elevators. What does a phobia feel like? When we react with illogical fear, become breathless and shaky and the heart beats fast. It is a frightening feeling. You are embarrassed and think people are watching you. You are apprehensive and afraid of going crazy, afraid of dying and afraid that something awful is going to happen.

It is the nature of man to have phobias and there is no explanation why. Some people are more phobic than others, depending on personality. Thinkers are more prone, and the more sensitive they are the more intense are their phobias. What causes them? Phobias are unreasonable fears and not to be confused with fears of fire, flood or accident. These are dangers linked to the fear facet of paranoia, our protective element. Phobias are brought on by traumatic experiences. We can develop them at any age and the degree to which they affect us depends on our emotional balance at the time. When this is upset, phobias are aggravated. There are times when they don't bother us, and they come and go for no apparent reason, but we can link their intensity to the amount of stress we are undergoing. Contributing factors to their development can be over indulgence in alcohol, the abuse of drugs, or excessive use of tranquilizers. They can also arise during depression.

A phobia can emerge out of the blue, with no relationship to an emotional shock. However, we can always connect it with an unpleasant experience, even though it may be foreign to the phobia. For example, suppose we speculate in the stock market and our losses are more than we can absorb. We blame ourselves and dwell upon this to the extent that it creates a fear of being hit by a car while crossing the street. This does not sound plausible, but it does happen.

Here is an example. Natalie, a child recently orphaned, went to live with her grandmother who was an austere and strict disciplinarian. The nine year old was forced to run errands to unlit parts of the house, and raced down the corridors in terror of the spirits chasing her. Her emotional imbalance from the loss of her parents created a fear of the dark which became a phobia. Another instance was about Jimmy. While learning to swim, he fell in over his head and swallowed a lot of water, resulting in a fear of deep water, and another about Sarah's big brother who loved to chase her around the house with a snake in one hand and worms in the other. To this day, Sarah has a dread of worms and snakes.

A phobia can be catching, as evidenced by George and his brother Ted. They both developed a phobia about spiders at a young age and, as small boys are rarely afraid of insects, where did this come from? It turned out that the parents employed a maid who became hysterical at the sight of a spider. Her phobia was picked up by the boys.

Can phobias be treated? Yes, there are three forms of treatment. Psychotherapy is the most successful, and can be supplemented by hypnosis. Then there is situational therapy by which the person is conditioned not to fear his phobia. For example, Karen was bitten by a dog and developed such a fear of dogs that she froze every time she saw one. Her distress was compounded by embarrassment, so she went for help. The therapist guided the conversation toward dogs, and soon she was able to talk about them. Then, he brought a puppy into the office and fondled it on his lap. He gradually persuaded her to touch it and she began to enjoy its cuddly playfulness. She was on the way to recovery.

William developed a dread of being in small spaces. His fear became so severe he had to plan his activities around it. Finally, he sought advice. Soon he was able to go with his therapist and take the elevator in an office building. Gradually, he made more frequent trips on elevators with his doctor, and later with his wife or a friend. Then he was able to go alone.

Group therapy is another form of therapy that is also effective for the treatment of phobias. There are phobia centers established around the country, and the results are excellent. Sharing problems with fellow sufferers hastens recovery.

Occasionally, phobias get out of hand. The sensitive thinking person is likely to develop a phobia so severe it requires professional help. In all cases the prognosis is excellent, and there is no reason to restrict lifestyle because of a phobia.

We can generate a phobia about anything and put a Greek name to it. Claustrophobia is the fear of closed in places, acrophobia of heights. Agoraphobia is the fear of open spaces, and has taken on the meaning of omniphobia, or fear of everything. There are people who fall into this category, whose phobias have multiplied to such an extent that they cover almost every situation, and they become, literally, prisoners in their homes.

INDEX

- Wed - Lease -

East Elm -

10 -

7 Benedict Pl.

Port Rd part Sibrity — light
Un Ponds — Light Right —
Part Ponds — End of Benedict
left side # 7 —
Turney + Whalen
- 661-9440 -
drumm or st parking -

Fanton - 935-8010 -